"The Art of Decision-Making is a pragmatic guide to sift out and get right the critical 1% in decisions at all levels. Based in real world practice, the book is a roadmap to a better system for decisions in your organisation."

— **Simon Terry**, Chairman, Bank First (Australia)

"Today's leaders deal with more complexity, uncertainty, and faster pace of change than ever before. This book stands out by distilling clear, actionable practices for the leaders who tackle those challenges head-on."

— **Tanja Ivkovic**, Partner, Heidrick & Struggles (Australia)

"A no-nonsense field guide to the decisions that actually matter. As AI commoditises execution, judgement on the critical few becomes the last real edge — and Maxim gives you the discipline to act on it. 100% beer, 0% froth."

— **Jonathan Silver**, CEO, Engage People Inc. (Canada)

"I often find business books formulaic, repetitive, and dry. Maxim's is the exception. It's practical and sharp — clearly written by someone who's been at the coalface of critical decisions and has a track record of success."

— **Paris Petranis**, Partner, K&L Gates (Australia)

"I've watched Maxim think through hard problems in real situations. The rigour and practicality in this book reflect how he actually works. The concepts in the book apply directly to both our own consulting team and the clients we work alongside. The mortal sins chapter alone is something I'd hand to a client before a major strategic decision, not after."

— **David Parsons**, CEO, Ellipsis (Australia)

"As we progress into the age of AI, decision-making will be one of the core skills that gives leaders the edge. The Art of Decision-Making provides a no-nonsense guide to those needing to make faster, better decisions. Written by someone with both consulting and real-world experience, this book is packed full of practical advice."

— **Dermot Crowley**, best-selling author and thought leader on productivity (Australia)

The Art of Decision-Making

The 50:1 Method for Nailing the Decisions that Define Success

Maxim Sharshun

The Art of Decision-Making

The 50:1 Method for Nailing the Decisions that Define Success

ISBN: 978-1-7646859-0-0
First published in Australia in 2026.

A catalogue record for this book is available from the National Library of Australia.

www.50-one.com

Disclaimers

This book is provided for general informational and educational purposes only and does not constitute professional advice. The author makes no warranties as to accuracy or suitability and accepts no liability for any loss or damage arising from its use.

Unless explicitly identified, the case studies, examples, and scenarios in this book are fictitious or fictionalised. Any resemblance to actual companies, organisations, or individuals is coincidental.

All trademarks, trade names, and product names referenced are the property of their respective owners and are used solely for identification and commentary. No sponsorship, endorsement, or affiliation is implied.

To my wife — my greatest coach and cheerleader...
and the best decision-maker in our household.

To my kids — who stretch me and teach me something
new every day.

To my parents — for the best launchpad in life
I could have asked for.

Contents

Preface ix

Part One. The Concept
Chapter 1: The Two Dimensions of Business 15
Chapter 2: Decision-Making and Strategy 29
Chapter 3: The 50:1 Rule 45
Chapter 4: The "1% To Die For" 57
Chapter 5: The Method of Nailing the 1% 69

Part Two. The Toolkit
Chapter 6: The "Who" 77
Chapter 7: The "How" 93
Chapter 8: The "Why" 115
Chapter 9: The "What" 133
Chapter 10: Decisions in Complex System 157

Part Three. The Practice
Chapter 11: Why Good Organisations Make Bad Decisions 177
Chapter 12: Leading Organisations from Good to Great 199

Epilogue 223

Preface

The one thing I find annoying about business and self-development literature is the amount of "filler", padding out the valuable insights. It's as if authors feel compelled to fill the book with 50,000 words, despite only having enough content for 5,000. It's a bit like having to work your way through three quarters of a pint of froth to get to the beer. However amazing that beer turns out to be, the experience is gone.

The promise I made to myself a while back was that if I was to ever write a book, it would be so densely packed with content that readers wouldn't want to miss a paragraph. 100% beer, 0% froth. My objective is to spare you the misery of having to wade through piles of filler in search of a rare insight. You'll be the judge if I succeed.

Another promise I made to myself was that this would be a no-nonsense book. I'm not an academic. Don't expect scientific evidence and piles of research behind the concepts I introduce. Everything I write about is grounded in real-world practice and, importantly, common sense. Unfortunately, common sense is becoming an endangered species in the corporate world, so this is a humble attempt to bring some of it back. The lessons and insights come from the hard-earned corporate battle scars, long nights cracking tough problems, and political manoeuvring to get stuff done without getting fired.

Throughout twenty-odd years of that, I developed an instinct for zeroing in on the critical path — the handful of calls that would make or break the outcome. It wasn't a conscious methodology. It was a survival mechanism, sharpened by 70-hour weeks in strategy consulting where working on the wrong thing meant working twice. MBA taught me the frameworks. Consulting taught me how to apply those. Hands-on industry work showed where frameworks break down. The combination produced a mental model I practised daily but never bothered to write down.

That changed in August 2019, when I posted a short LinkedIn article on what I called the 50:1 rule. It resonated more than I expected. A year later I followed up with a piece on identifying the «1% to die in the ditch for», which received good feedback too. A few friends and colleagues suggested I write a book. I resisted — I didn't want to add to the pile of business books that should be one-page brochures. I started reluctantly in 2024 and finished in 2026. What you're holding is the result: twenty years of practice, compressed into a method I wish someone had handed me on day one.

This book is written for everyone who makes or influences consequential decisions as part of their job — from board members setting strategic direction, to senior executives leading business divisions and driving transformation, to subject matter experts whose analysis and recommendations underpin critical choices. The bigger the decisions at stake, the more valuable the toolkit proposed in this book becomes.

There are many examples of both good and imperfect decision-making in this book. Many without making reference to specific companies. This is deliberate. The book is not about shaming organisations or individuals. The purpose is to demonstrate how important it is to have strong discipline in making deliberate calls, and how powerful (negatively or positively) the effects of decision-making can be.

These case studies are simplified examples of complex situations. And as with any complex situation, if you had three people involved, you'd get four different stories. So, to avoid upsetting anybody, treat all exemplars provided in this book as fictional ones, which may or may not have been inspired by real-world situations.

Trigger warning. If you've spent any time in management consulting or reading business books, you'll have been conditioned to expect everything in threes. Three strategic priorities. Three pillars. Three horizons. I know that it's neat, memorable, and fits nicely on a PowerPoint slide. I regret to inform you that this book does not comply. The core framework has four elements (Who, How, Why, and What). The cultural operating system has four pillars (Focus, Openness, Clarity, and Speed). The failure patterns come in sixes: the mortal sins and key cognitive biases. The no-nonsense promise stopped me from forcing everything into threes. If you've been wired the other way, my sincere apologies. You'll adjust — it's worth it.

No business book coming onto the market misses an opportunity to mention AI. This one will not be an exception. By the time you read this, AI will have made another leap. It can summarise a hundred-page report in seconds, model scenarios that would take a team of analysts weeks, and brainstorm strategic options that sound remarkably plausible. None of that changes the core thesis of this book. AI is an exceptional co-pilot, which can help by processing vast troves of information, brainstorming options, or narrowing down the analytical problems. What it can't (yet) do is frame the right question, weigh incommensurable trade-offs, or carry the conviction to commit when the data runs out. The "1%" decisions that disproportionately determine success or failure remain stubbornly human. This book is about building the discipline, culture, and judgement to get those right, which I argue is more an art than a science. AI will make you faster and better informed, but it won't make the hard calls for you... or at least not yet.

Chapter 12 starts with the quote from a Polish-American Olympic weightlifter and poet, Jerzy Gregorek, who once said: "Hard choices, easy life. Easy choices, hard life". Eight words that capture the essence of this book. The 50:1 rule that we will touch a few times throughout the book is all about hyperfocused decision-making — concentrating effort on the small fraction of choices that deliver extraordinary leverage, and deliberately letting go of the rest. The organisations and leaders who consistently face into those difficult calls — early, with an open mind, and with courage — build momentum that makes everything downstream easier. Those who duck them, defer them, or dilute them pay the hefty price later.

A word on structure. The book introduces the 50:1 Method in three parts. The first five chapters set the scene: what decision-making actually is, why it matters more than most leaders think, and where to focus your finite attention. The core concept here is the 50:1 Rule that identifies which decisions deserve your best effort. The second part includes five chapters that unpack the Who, How, Why, and What toolkit of making consequential decisions well, along with a practical approach to structuring complex, interdependent choices. The third part includes the final two chapters that diagnose the most common failure patterns and offer a treatment plan for fixing them.

Like a fine dining degustation, the book is designed to be consumed in the order directed by the chef. Each chapter builds on the last, the case studies land better when read in order, and the occasional callback rewards those who've been paying attention.

That said, not everyone has the patience for a twelve-course meal. If you'd rather skip straight to dessert and start with the method in chapters 6 through 10, go for it. The frameworks are practical enough to stand on their own, and you can always circle back for the context later.

You will also notice that certain concepts are addressed in multiple chapters. That's deliberate. The ex-consultant in me wanted to eliminate every repetition, but the author in me wanted each chapter to stand on its own so you can jump straight to the method, revisit a framework, or dip into a topic without needing to re-read everything that came before. The author won.

Part One

The Concept

Chapter 1:
The Two Dimensions of Business

"Whenever you see a successful business, someone once made a courageous decision."

— PETER DRUCKER

Compass vs Engine

First, let's get one thing straight: any organisation exists by doing just two things — deciding and executing. That's it. Every profit, loss, customer win, failed transformation or culture survey result ultimately links back to how well you do those two things. Either you made the right call, or you didn't. Either you delivered on it, or you didn't.

The challenge with this is that companies treat execution like a science, and decision-making like a natural instinct that senior leaders possess by definition. We pour time and money into agile delivery, Lean Six Sigma, change and project management, and governance. We invest in operating model redesigns and culture transformations. But when it comes to making critical calls? We wing it, shirk it, overcomplicate the obvious, get stuck in analysis paralysis, ignore what matters most, or revisit the same decision multiple times.

AI is transforming how organisations execute. It can optimise logistics, personalise customer interactions, automate workflows, and flag data anomalies that would take a human team months to spot. Where it falls short is on the decisions that matter most. The consequential choices that shape the future of a business involve far more than the propensity models and pattern recognition that underpin AI algorithms. Those models are trained on historical data. They are good at telling us what is likely to happen if the world continues to behave the way it has before. But the critical decisions are almost always about the future that doesn't look like the past: entering a new market, reshaping a business model, making a bet on an unproven technology. These involve judgement calls that no amount of historical data can resolve.

From an organisational perspective, decision-making is the compass; execution is the engine. It doesn't matter how powerful the engine is, or how fast the organisation is moving; if it's heading south when it should be going north — you'll just get further off track.

As AI matures, it is making the engine exponentially more powerful. In just a couple of years, the technology shifted from a novelty for tech enthusiasts to a tool that now delivers a substantial share of software development and testing. Marketing assets that once took months to produce can be created in hours. Complex data analytics tasks that used to take weeks of expert work can now be produced by generalists in minutes. The same acceleration will ripple across many other disciplines. But as the ngine gets more powerful, the importance of a reliable compass increases too. An organisation that is delivering at speed but heading slightly off-track will find that competitors can close the gap in no time. The faster you can go, the more careful you need to be in ensuring that you are going in the right direction.

Nailing decisions delivers the highest Return on Invested Effort. Most leaders and organisations spend only a fraction of their time in "decision-making mode" compared to "execution mode", yet in my experience, the respective contributions of the two modes to success are roughly equal. We'll unpack how to get 50x return on your effort with the radical 50:1 Rule in chapter 3.

Unfortunately, the boundary between execution and decision-making is not clear-cut. It often depends on both the challenge you're facing and where you sit in the organisation. What counts as execution for one leader is decision-making for another.

What Is a Decision?

Bear with me for a few paragraphs of theory. It's the only stretch in the book where I lean on scholars rather than scars — but a working definition is worth it before we use the word 'decision' another thousand times.

As Warren B. Powell, Professor at Princeton University, puts it in his article What is a decision? (and how do we make them), "Decisions are a fundamental human activity, studied and debated throughout our entire history, driven by our endless desire to improve".

A stricter definition comes from Ron Howard's 1966 paper: "A decision is an irrevocable allocation of resources, irrevocable in the sense that it is impossible or extremely costly to change back to the situation that existed before making the decision. Thus, for our purposes, a decision is not a mental commitment to follow a course of action but rather the actual pursuit of that course of action".

A somewhat less strict definition is from David Skinner's Introduction to Decision Analysis (3rd edition): "A decision is a conscious course of action and allocation of resources to achieve a stated set of objectives".

We could go as far back as Aristotle (~350 BCE), for whom a decision was "a deliberate choice of action made through reasoning, aimed at achieving a good or virtuous end".

The two problems I see with the above definitions are that they imply (1) a deliberate choice is being made and (2) resources are involved. While this is true in most cases, it unnecessarily constrains the scope. In my view, even when "decisions" are made on autopilot, without realising that a choice is being made (more on this in chapter 4), they are still decisions. Resource restriction is a bit more flexible. Even spending ten minutes drafting an email to an unhappy customer could be considered a commitment made off the back of a decision to deal with an issue rather than let it slide.

> *For the purposes of this book, let's make our own simple and broad definition of decision, taking Skinner's one as a basis:*
> **"A decision is choosing a consequential course of action to achieve a stated set of objectives".**
> *The word "consequential" is added to filter out any trivial daily choices that don't have a meaningful impact on the outcome. Say you need to get to an important client meeting to finalise a deal. You can choose how to get there — by Uber, taxi, bus, or metro. While the objective of landing a deal is important, the method of transport to the client's office (as long as it's on time) is inconsequential.*

Before the CEO and executive team enter the picture, the board has already shaped the playing field — setting the growth ambition and risk appetite for the business, and determining the capital structure: how much to return to shareholders versus reinvest.

Then the CEO of the enterprise can decide what targets to set and how to allocate available capital between the "core" business and a new venture — let's call it NewCo. For the CEO, delivering against those targets within the board's guardrails becomes execution.

But for the group executive leading NewCo, those targets and budgets trigger a string of strategic choices. They might, for example, choose to go all-in on a single business line and pause other opportunities — trading diversification for a high-risk, high-reward play. The General Manager running this prioritised business line will then face a new set of decisions about how to hit those targets with the capital on hand. For the NewCo executive, that's execution. For the General Manager, there are a series of decisions to be made.

That context dependence and shifting perspective is part of what makes decision-making more art than science. Execution must be efficient and predictable. Decision-making requires judgement, trade-offs, and the ability to act under uncertainty. And like any art, it must be mastered. It doesn't happen magically when someone is promoted. This book was written to help leaders and companies develop this muscle and use it deliberately.

FIGURE 1.1: DECISION-MAKING HIERARCHY

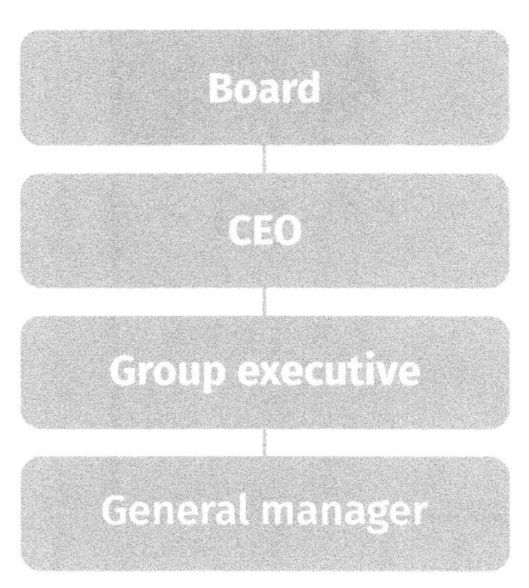

Surely, you may say, execution matters just as much. Of course, excellence in setting direction is never a substitute for excellence in delivery. Both elements are essential for success. Neither alone is sufficient. High-performing execution requires many elements working in sync. It must be efficient — that is, without wasting time or resources. It must be consistent and repeatable — not based on luck. It must come with clear responsibilities and governance. It also needs to be adequately funded and enabled by the right capabilities, be it people, processes or technology. As the following chapters will show, similar requirements apply to effective decision-making.

However, no matter how great your ways of working are, they can't fix a flawed direction. You can't "deliver" your way out of a series of bad choices. And that's why decision-making must be viewed as a core leadership craft that requires ongoing development and refinement.

From Mediocre Majority to Unicorns

To bring the distinction between execution and decision-making to life, here's a simple two-by-two that unpacks where different companies fit.

FIGURE 1.2: DECISION-MAKING VS EXECUTION

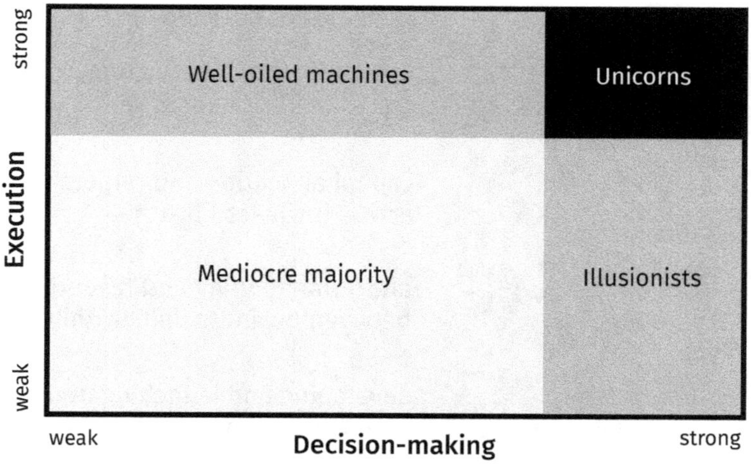

*First, there are the **Unicorns** — rare companies that consistently make the right business calls and deliver. They're fast and focused. They don't have to be perfect, but they get the big calls right and execute with discipline, which in most cases translates to above-market performance. Let's not call names, but I'm sure you've heard of companies that generate exceptional shareholder returns, perform strongly in their core business and successfully expand into new adjacencies.*

*Then there are the **Illusionists.** These companies are great at strategy decks, investor pitches, blue-sky thinking, and innovation theatre. But when it comes to follow-through? It all falls apart. All sizzle, no sausage. We've all heard about those once-hyped companies that sold the dream through clear and compelling world-changing narratives, then destroyed billions in value through sloppy execution.*

*Next, the **Well-Oiled Machines.** They hit metrics, run tight operations, and manage delivery risk. But they rarely challenge themselves, and often miss the inflection points. Their problem isn't execution — it's decision-making. They can still be good at making certain calls, but that's contained to their comfort* *zone of core business — not a fully mastered craft. Some large industrial, energy and mining businesses would fit into that category. There are plenty of examples of energy or mining majors venturing into new sectors only to quietly pull out few years later.*

*And then there's the **Mediocre Majority**. Lots of good companies are stuck in mediocrity-land. These are not quite nailing either dimension.*

This book will provide insights and tools to help you make a shift to the right.

When the Compass Fails

Most organisations don't suffer from a lack of ideas. Quite the opposite, they suffer from a lack of clarity about which ideas and choices matter. Too often direction gets lost in abstraction. We've all seen leaders using what I'd call "question-speak", a series of smart-sounding high-level questions that lack substance and aren't remotely helpful in direction setting.

Another challenge is that leaders gravitate to solving the problems they understand, not the ones that count — then teams follow. Hard calls get avoided, decision debt piles up, and deadlines crumble under pressure. Then everything becomes urgent. Amidst urgency, it's even less clear what's important. When everything is a priority — nothing is. Sounds familiar?

There are many ways in which a lack of decision-making discipline may manifest in an organisation. Product features get descoped or added without considering upstream and downstream impact. Minor issues get escalated to the senior leadership team, while existential ones remain hidden in the PowerPoint footnotes. Meetings are held to socialise issues without any decisions being made, and everyone leaves with a different understanding of "where to from here". I'm sure you could name another dozen examples. All of this costs time, energy, and trust. We will discuss some of the common pitfalls in more detail in chapter 11.

When leaders stumble into important decisions, the criticality of those decisions is not always obvious. So, it's not uncommon to see those ending up being a captain's call in the corridor, or an abstract consensus at a haphazard meeting where everyone comes out with what they wanted to hear, but no real clarity. Or, my personal favourite, a groupthink-approved compromise option — one no one cares to object to, but no one actually believes in either.

Despite its challenges, this direction-setting aspect of leadership is attractive to many. Having the authority to make calls that shape the organisation's future is one of the reasons why people seek career growth. However, it's also an area where it is not easy to objectively measure effectiveness, but it is easy to overestimate one's own abilities.

Let's be blunt — many leaders dramatically overestimate how good they are at decision-making. But isn't making the right calls what the leaders are paid big bucks for? Their track record of choices is what they got promoted for. How can they not be great at that?

Instead of getting into trouble for commenting on the corporate promotions (which are decisions themselves, wink-wink), let me reveal the biggest secret of the book upfront. Too many leaders (and their teams) operate in a haze of blind decisions — calls made on the fly, often without even realising that a decision is made, and certainly without framing or awareness of the potential consequences. Sometimes, a blind decision actually means NOT making a decision where one is required. Look around you — these are everywhere.

As Daniel Kahneman explains in his book Thinking, Fast and Slow (2011) our brains are wired for efficiency. We constantly use mental shortcuts — heuristics — to ind fast and simple answers. He calls it System 1 (fast) thinking. In many situations, this is not only helpful, it's necessary. If we had to consciously evaluate every choice we face, we'd be cognitively overwhelmed, if not paralysed.

The problems arise when those shortcuts bleed into high-stakes business calls — strategic trade-offs, product design, regulatory interpretation. Those calls require deliberate and analytical System 2 (slow) thinking. We will look at how biases and heuristics impact our ability to make the right calls in chapter 11.

There could be many reasons for leaders to miss those major choices. In my experience, the most common one is assuming that something is an execution matter rather than a choice to be made. Imagine a financial services organisation that invested three years into building a proprietary methodology for determining customers' financial wellbeing. When this company decides to implement a digital platform to deliver financial education and advice programs to its customers, it's natural to assume that the financial wellbeing methodology should be built into the new platform. The company made a major investment and wants to show the payoff. If the new platform allows the methodology to be implemented out-of-the-box, it's fine to classify it as part of execution. But if implementation requires a year of additional development and testing, then it becomes a highly consequential scope choice. The defence that "we've invested three years" doesn't cut it.

The other reason for missing could be a misunderstanding of the importance of choice. In our example above, the leaders may be assuming that integration is a trivial task. I've seen lots of epic stuff-ups stemming from this "How hard can it be?" line of thinking.

When inconsequential choices get botched, no one may notice, but when consequential decisions are made unconsciously, it could dramatically impact organisational performance. If we don't identify them, frame them, and evaluate their implications, we risk drifting into disasters we could've avoided.

In a case study below, a seemingly trivial decision to remove a piece of the matching algorithm to save a few days of effort nearly led to an operational crisis. What was missed? Not just a few lines of code — but the recognition that this small detail was on the critical path. The team executed well. But they were heading in the wrong direction.

The Descoping Disaster

A large superannuation administrator called in consultants to review a multi-million-dollar project. The goal was to integrate its administration platform with a new government clearing house, automating superannuation contributions for millions of Australians and hundreds of thousands of businesses.

Launch was just a couple of months away. One of the executives had a nagging feeling something wasn't right. So, two strategy consultants — green, eager, and totally unfamiliar with the superannuation technology — were asked to take a look.

They were out of their depth. Superannuation contributions? Digital clearing houses? But they did the only sensible thing: found a couple of senior IT leaders and a veteran from operations, who agreed to join a working session.

Together they started mapping out project risks — past issues, scope changes, potential pain points. It looked like a solid list. Most of the risks were manageable: minor financial impacts, maybe a few extra FTEs to mop up edge cases and exceptions.

Then they got to one line item: "Advanced matching algorithm".

It had been casually cut from scope during a Steering Committee meeting, part of a broader time-saving push to claw back a slipping timeline. "Advanced" sounded like a luxury — some gold plating the business could live without.

Until they unpacked the implications.

The "basic" version of the algorithm couldn't handle franchised employers — fast food chains, petrol stations, retail store networks, gyms or other franchise holders. These employers use nested business identifiers that the government's standard didn't account for.

What that meant was that tens of thousands of contributions would fail to reconcile. Every single month. For every single franchisee. The system would create duplicate accounts for hundreds of thousands of superannuation members.

When they asked how long it would take to manually fix them, the operations lead looked grim. "If we stopped all other work," she said, "it would take us three months just to clean up one month of errors."

What looked like a time-saving tweak turned out to be an operational dead-end. Thankfully, the business still had time to reverse the decision and reinstate the advanced matching logic. It replicated a multi-step manual process that the operations team had perfected over years — now baked into the code.

A two-week shortcut nearly caused a full-blown operational and reputational crisis.

At the time, dropping what seemed to be a "nice-to-have" feature probably felt like good delivery discipline. But the decision was made without clarity, without curiosity, and without proper input. It was fast, reactive — and blind.

The Role of Leadership

Peter Drucker, the father of modern management, once observed: *"Only three things happen naturally in organisations: friction, confusion, and underperformance. Everything else requires leadership"*. His point is blunt: clarity, alignment, and disciplined decision-making don't just appear on their own. Left to their own devices, organisations default to busywork and optics management.

At the heart of Drucker's observation is human nature. People are wired to seek validation and avoid embarrassment. Praise and recognition feed our ego and social standing — instincts that once determined our place in the tribe. Equally, fear of failure or humiliation triggers the same primal response that once signalled danger of being cast out, with survival at stake. In modern organisations, those instincts haven't disappeared — they've just evolved into safer, more polished and politically correct forms.

Unfortunately, some leaders choose the wrong options: they take credit and avoid responsibility. They seek recognition, and play it carefully to protect their image. Often, this is not down to malice, it's simply psychology at work. If left unchecked, this "psychology" breeds exactly what Drucker warned about: friction, confusion, and underperformance.

Therefore, the key job of a leader is not simply to allocate tasks and maintain order, but to actively set direction, cut through the noise, and create the conditions for making good choices and getting stuff done. Building those conditions almost always means overcoming deeply ingrained instincts — the pull to seek credit and the tendency to avoid responsibility when outcomes are uncertain. Effective leaders consciously design cultures where truth is valued over ego and progress over optics, where people feel safe to own outcomes rather than protect status.

When it comes to execution, leaders' roles are well understood. They focus much of their effort on fostering an environment where teams can reliably deliver the best outcomes for the organisation and its customers. Lots of good books are written on this topic.

However, when it comes to decision-making, the role of leadership may not be as obvious. Is it about authority and delegation? Or about creating an environment where the right people make the decisions? Or about making decisions effectively? Or maybe about clarity as to which decisions to make in the first place? Well, the issue is that the answer is — "all of the above".

It's not a matter of just drafting a new all-encompassing RACI (a roles-and-responsibilities matrix popular in large corporates) or training the team to use a hypothesis-driven approach (known as HDA in management consulting) in problem-solving. That's why it's taking me a couple of hundred pages to bring the holistic method to life.

As we will uncover throughout the book, effective decision-making is much more about clarity, and less about control. Clarity as to "who" and "how" is something we'll explore in chapters 6 and 7. Leaders don't need to make every call themselves. Quite the opposite, actually. But they need to ensure the *right calls* are made, by the *right people*, with the *right context*, at the *right time*.

An effective leader needs to play the role of radar and clearing house for the few decisions that matter most. In the days before modern navigation technology, a ship crossing the Arctic Ocean relied on a lookout watching for icebergs. Organisations are no different — they need leaders looking out for consequential choices that can't be left to happen organically. Once an "iceberg" is located, the team needs to be alerted to navigate around it. The leader needs to ensure the matter gets the attention it deserves, and the call is well thought through. We'll get to the "why" and "what" — which outline the process of defining the objectives, asking the right questions, and tackling those — in chapters 8 and 9.

The other critical job for a leader is coaching the team and the broader organisation on navigating complex decisions on their own. There's no better way of coaching than leading by example. And yet so many leaders get it wrong. We've probably all come across those who defer critical decisions until it's too late or get stuck in an analysis-paralysis loop. Some obsess about inconsequential matters or those they are most familiar with. Others jump the gun by making fast, ill-informed calls on high-stakes choices. These are just a few of the senior leaders' sins.

We explore those as well as some solutions in more detail in chapters 11 and 12.

This book is all about building the discipline. You'll learn how to spot the moments when a decision will make or break your outcome, how to cut through complexity without oversimplifying, and how to build decision-making capability not just within yourself, but within your whole organisation. The goal is to give you a reliable compass, so that when you power up the engine, you know you're heading in the right direction.

The next chapter dives deeper into the interplay between decision-making and strategy as well as the consequences of organisations making bad choices.

Chapter 2:
Decision-Making and Strategy

"The essence of strategy is choosing what not to do."

— MICHAEL PORTER

Strategy and Decision-Making

Some may be curious about why this book contrasts "decision-making" with execution rather than "strategy" with execution. Fair question. Let's work through it.

One of the cleanest and most pragmatic definitions of strategy is from a book Playing to Win: How Strategy Really Works (Harvard Business Review Press, 2013) by A.G. Lafley and Roger L. Martin.

> *"Strategy is a coherent set of choices about where to play, how to win, and how to sustain advantage over time".*

Lafley (former CEO of Procter & Gamble) and Martin (then Dean of Rotman School of Management) use it as the foundation for their "Playing to Win" framework, which has been widely adopted in both corporates and consulting circles.

However, there's a golden nugget that I have put at the beginning of the chapter header from Michael Porter (What is Strategy, 1996). He argues that true strategy requires sacrifice, choice, and trade-offs. The most important bit to add is this: "The essence of strategy is choosing what not to do".

So "strategy" is a set of decisions or choices, importantly, covering what not to do! This strategic set of choices sits at the tip of the iceberg. However, as we'll unpack in the subsequent chapters, it's insufficient for a company to nail just that tip. If a hypothetical business made perfect decisions on which markets to enter and which capabilities to develop and products to sell, while botching the next level of detail such as product features, pricing, customer support model, go-to-market choices, and so on, its chances of success aren't great.

Yes, companies need to make good strategic choices, but the decision-making discipline must encompass everything they do — from once-in-a-decade plant expansion choices to daily improvements in customer support.

When things aren't going well, many organisations think "we need better strategy" when what they really need is better decisions at all levels.

AMP's "Customer-Centric" Strategy That Wasn't

In the years leading up to the Royal Commission, AMP — one of Australia's most prominent wealth management companies — promoted itself as a champion of «customer centricity». The words appeared in strategy decks, leadership speeches, and glossy brochures. The company had a brilliant strategy: put the customer at the heart of every decision, and Funds Under Management would grow.

But the Royal Commission into Misconduct in the Banking, Superannuation and Financial Services Industry (2017–2019) found that day-to-day choices were anything but customer-centric. When the business faced commercial choices, the system leaned towards "financial planner centricity" — ensuring that the interests of country's largest licensed planner network were protected. When it came to products, the default was "profit centricity" — choices that maximised returns even if it happened at the expense of transparency or fairness.

This gap between stated strategy and lived decision-making grew wider over time. Regulators eventually stepped in, exposing misconduct that had been festering under the veneer of "customer centricity". The Royal Commission identified that AMP engaged in severe misconduct such as charging fees for no service, its advisers providing inappropriate advice, paying and receiving prohibited commissions, and making misrepresentations to the regulator.

AMP went from a top-20 listed Australian company with a $30 billion market capitalisation in 2001 to a $3 billion mid-market player 20 years later.

The lesson from AMP's experience during the Royal Commission era is clear: «customer centric» strategy is only as real as the systems, incentives, and guardrails that force every decision to serve the customer first.

Two ends of the strategy spectrum

At its core, strategy boils down to choices about how to play the game. And those choices tend to sit between two extremes of a strategy spectrum:

1) Play safe and keep nailing the core.

This is the conservative end. It's about avoiding bad calls, sticking to what works, and doubling down on the fundamentals. Think of it as the "steady rally" game plan — keep the ball in play, minimise errors, and win by being more consistent than your opponent. That's actually where a lot of "well-oiled machines" from chapter 1 would sit.

2) Play bold and explore the boundaries of the possible.

This is the opposite end. It's about stretching into new territory — whether that's technology, regulation, or business models — to capture value others are too cautious to chase. Here, you win by taking risks that competitors shy away from, pushing into the edges where the rules aren't fully written yet. That's the territory of "Unicorns".

This spectrum isn't limited to business — it shows up everywhere: in life, in politics, in sports. Some tennis players grind at the baseline, forcing their rivals into tiring rallies until they eventually make a mistake. Others charge the net, disrupt rhythm, and win by taking bold shots. Both approaches can work. Both require skill and discipline.

Solid decision-making is important at either end of the spectrum. But the magnitude of importance and the way decisions get made differs. In bold plays, which demand the courage to embrace risk, paired with the discipline to avoid reckless bets, decision-making is absolutely critical to survival. In conservative plays, which demand vigilance to avoid unforced errors and complacency, good decisions help to stay on track.

Strategic leadership is about figuring out where your organisation should sit on this spectrum, and then applying the right decision-making approach for that position. Too cautious, and you miss opportunities. Too reckless, and you burn capital and credibility. The balance and the ability to shift when conditions change is what separates resilient leaders from the rest.

The Play-Safe Strategy

To save you $100k in MBA fees and years of management consulting grind, I'll reveal a secret. The most reliable business and life strategy is to simply not do dumb stuff!

In most sectors, companies don't need to "outsmart" and "outmanoeuvre" competitors; they can successfully compete by just steering a steady course and avoiding bad decisions. Yes, it's that simple. For some businesses, this strategy can even take them to the top of the scoreboard.

The central risk of the "play-safe" strategy is getting distracted by "dead wood" opportunities, which divert resources from those that yield real results. Those bad decisions often arise from sunk cost bias, coupled with the vanity factor and, sometimes, the personal attachment of senior stakeholders, which can perpetuate waste and starve the "winners". We'll talk more about biases in chapter 11.

The companies that get it wrong allocate resources through compromise where all business units get something. Unable to make tough calls, organisations scatter resources thinly across a wide range of initiatives, some keeping the lights on, others strengthening the core, and many chasing innovation opportunities. The outcome is an enterprise portfolio by osmosis, which relies more on political balancing than on deliberate decision-making. As a result, the core does not get enough to prosper, and a plethora of innovation initiatives get barely enough to survive. A better resource allocation under this strategy would be to bias heavily towards a few initiatives that deliver value and allocate only a small portion of capital to a couple of high-conviction innovation and experimentation opportunities — the fewer and more focused, the better. But this transition does not happen organically — it requires difficult conversations and deliberate trade-offs.

FIGURE 2.1: PLAY-SAFE ENTERPRISE PORTFOLIO

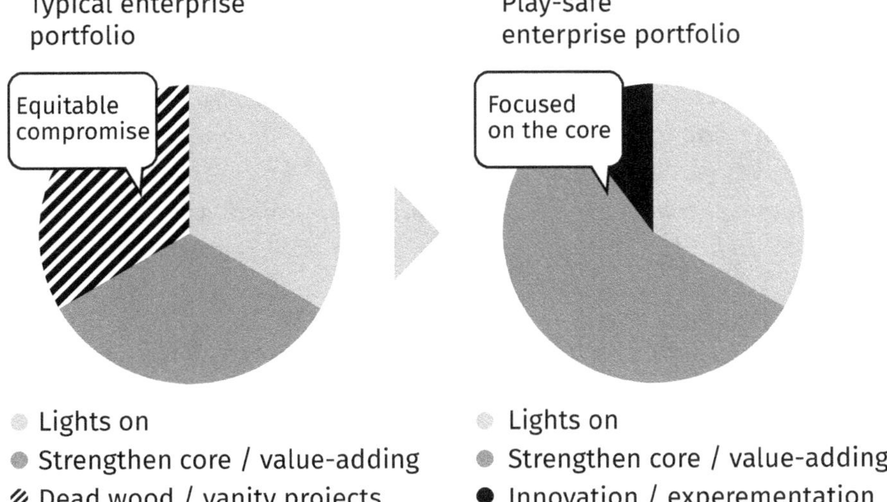

The ability to focus is one of the most valuable and probably underrated leadership skills. It is essential to good decision-making, which, as we now know, is essential to success. From an enterprise perspective, investment in innovation and experimentation with uncertain outcomes is critical to stay competitive in the long term. However, to succeed, leaders need to be ruthless about killing lots of "good ideas" without delay or regret and doubling down on the few "best" ones.

The same strategy can apply to our personal lives. Double down on what's important to you and avoid doing things just to please others or manage optics.

Apple's Overextension Before Jobs' Return

In the mid-1990s, Apple was in serious trouble. Once a pioneer of personal computing, the company had lost focus. Rather than doubling down on its core strengths, Apple had expanded its portfolio far beyond what it could manage. The product line became bloated with dozens of models and sub-variants of Macintosh computers, along with printers, digital cameras, and even game consoles. Each new launch was meant to capture another niche, but instead, it spread resources thin, confused customers, and created massive operational complexity.

For consumers, the range was overwhelming. Two machines sitting side by side in a store often differed only marginally, leaving customers puzzled. For developers and partners, the fragmentation created compatibility issues and diluted the once-tight Apple ecosystem. Internally, engineering teams were pulled in too many directions, and the company lacked the discipline to say no.

Financial performance mirrored the chaos. Apple's market share eroded steadily, its products struggled to stand out, and losses mounted. By 1997, the company was on the brink of bankruptcy. Analysts and media speculated openly about its collapse or sale.

When Steve Jobs returned that year, he famously slashed the product line by 70%, cutting it down to just four categories: a desktop and a laptop, each for consumers and professionals. He forced the organisation to focus its talent and energy where it could truly differentiate. That decision set the foundation for Apple's turnaround and eventual dominance.

Overextension is seductive but can be deadly for the business. Expanding beyond capacity creates complexity, misalignment, and drains scarce resources. The discipline of focus — saying no to most things and stopping what doesn't work — is often the hardest decision, but it is the one that saves companies from drifting into irrelevance.

The Play-Bold Strategy

If avoiding dumb choices keeps you in the game, making bold moves is how you change the game. It's not about bravado, but about asymmetric bets — moves where the upside significantly outweighs the downside once you've done the work to contain the risk. Bold decisions push into new tech, new business models, or new regulatory ground to create value competitors are too slow or too cautious to pursue.

Another thing to keep in mind is that bold does not mean reckless. Reckless is a leap without a clear plan. Bold is a sequenced commitment: you plan carefully, mitigate or manage known risks, and then commit and implement decisively. The rhythm is something like: probe → learn fast → scale. When leaders hesitate after the learning phase, organisations stall in the pilot mode. When they skip the learning phase, they burn capital on avoidable mistakes. The success depends on knowing when the evidence is strong enough and conviction is high to move from reversible probes to a decisive scale-up.

Organisations that pursue bold strategies still need to ensure that their core business is sufficiently funded to deliver sustainable returns. But once the basics are covered, they should bias all available enterprise resources towards one big bet — the one that is expected to deliver a disproportionate long-term payoff. It does not mean that there is only one major opportunity that an organisation can ever pursue — just one at a time. Playing bold requires a significant shift in resource allocation — which is almost always a complex and politically charged decision.

Three disciplines separate effective boldness from innovation drama.

First, maintain razor-sharp focus. No company can effectively pursue multiple big, bold bets at once while keeping the core business humming. To maximise the chances of success, pick one big battle at a time. Staying focused while pursuing the bold strategy also requires killing or parking numerous good ideas along the way — without regret or hesitation. Jeff Bezos in one of his interviews quoted a piece of advice from his mentor, Jeff Wilke, who said, "Jeff, you have enough ideas — per minute, per day, per week — to destroy Amazon. You have to release the work at the right rate, so that the organisation can accept it". These big and bold moves need to come at a sustainable pace to get enough attention and energy to escape corporate and market gravity and lift off to the orbit.

FIGURE 2.2: PLAY-BOLD ENTERPRISE PORTFOLIO

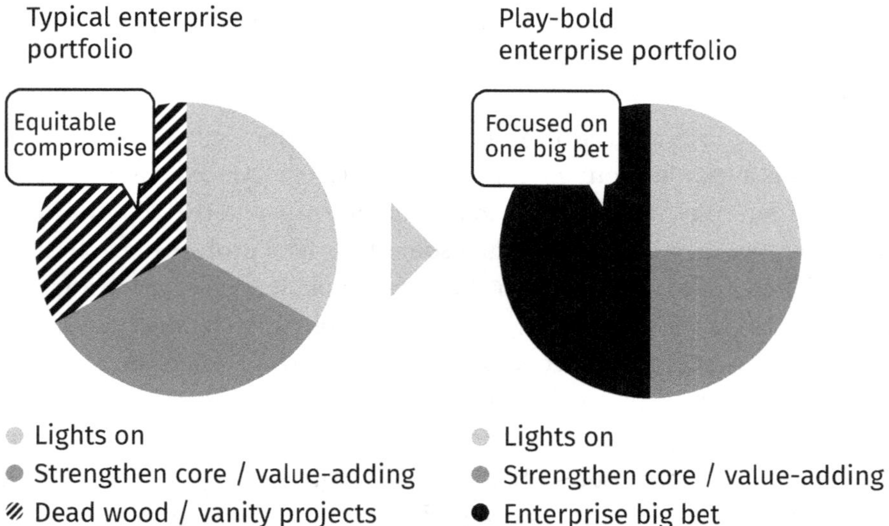

Then, set clear boundaries and destination. The strategy needs to clearly define the non-negotiables up front (customer harm, regulatory red lines, capex limits). If the bet comes close to crossing them, stop or redesign. Equally important is to set unambiguous go/no-go criteria. Decide in advance what evidence will stop the bet and what will trigger scale. No moving goalposts.

Finally, ensure ownership and resourcing. Put your A-grade talent on the bet and remove the friction (funding, architecture bottlenecks, governance drag, and so on) that quietly kills momentum.

Bold plays need to explicitly call out assumptions that carry most of the value (e.g. adoption curve, unit economics at scale, regulatory pathway). Attack those assumptions first with the cheapest tests available — analysis, expert conversations, tiny market experiments — and only make tangible commitments (hiring, capex, partnerships) when the belief is justified. We'll look at this in more detail in chapter 8.

Finally, bold strategy demands alignment and courage. You've got to align your board and team around why this is the right call now — and what you'll do if it doesn't work out. That may include a public "change of mind" plan. There is no shame in pivoting when facts change; the shame is in doubling down to save face. We will discuss alignment and courage to pivot in more detail in chapter 12.

Breaking All Boundaries at Once

Uber is a textbook case. Founded in 2009, it wasn't just launching a new app. It broke through three frontiers at once:
- *Technology: using GPS-enabled smartphones for real-time ride matching.*
- *Business model: scaling a peer-to-peer platform where drivers used their own vehicles.*
- *Regulation: entering markets where taxi licensing rules had stood unchallenged for decades.*

Each decision was bold — not just because of the idea, but because Uber committed visibly. They launched aggressively into city after city, knowing regulators would resist. They mobilised customer support to pressure policymakers. They invested heavily in driver recruitment and incentives to build two-sided liquidity quickly. The downside was severe: lawsuits, bans, even potential shutdowns. But the upside — global dominance in personal transport — was game-changing.

The end result is well known: despite legal battles, Uber reshaped mobility worldwide, became a verb, and built a multi-billion-dollar enterprise.

Few companies would want to follow Uber's bold moves and the regulatory battles that come with it. However, it's important to understand the mechanics of bold decision-making. We take a deep dive into the frameworks that will help navigate those questions in chapters 8 and 9.

Used well, bold plays compress years of incrementalism into quarters of step-change. Used poorly, they become vanity projects that suck the life out of business. The difference isn't luck — it's discipline and leadership that knows when to push, when to pause, and when to pull back.

The Cost of Bad Decisions

The AMP example shows that the implications of poor choices over long periods can be catastrophic. There are plenty of cases that show various dimensions of this. Some are driven by failure of governance decisions, such as Enron, Arthur Andersen, and more recently PwC, others due to poor strategic and commercial decisions such as Kodak, Blockbuster, and Nokia.

Those headline-grabbing cases get a lot of attention; however, I would argue they are just a drop in the ocean of bad decisions. The ocean itself is made of a vast range of daily poor choices that happen without notice across most organisations. These daily poor choices act like sand in the gearbox — creating friction, wearing the system (and people) down, and in the long run leading to failures.

Let me share a couple of examples.

A Trivial Choice That Almost Cost Hundreds of Thousands

As part of a digital health service development, the team was building an API to let customers use a mobile app to see if a particular service was available to them as part of their insurance cover at no cost.

The simple tech solution design that the team proposed would return a binary answer — "yes" (no cost) or "no" (fee applies). The specification came from the pilot requirements, which allowed one free service per year. Everyone assumed the rules would remain unchanged.

Midway through design, a question surfaced during a corridor conversation: "What if a customer has three eligible services included in their product, one is used, but two are still available for free? How do we show that in the app?" Silence followed. Nobody had considered the post-pilot requirements. The team had locked into the pilot logic and designed the solution accordingly.

Luckily, the gap was caught early. Extending the solution to return "X still available out of Y included services" added only a couple of hours of work for developers and testers. If the flaw had been discovered after launch, the technology would have required rebuilding a few months down the track. By then, the revision would have taken at least a couple of fortnightly sprints — resulting in hundreds of thousands of dollars of avoidable effort, plus delivery delays.

Just one "small" decision. How many similar choices get made daily — quietly, unconsciously, and never corrected? Multiply these across thousands of teams and projects (not only in the technology space), and it's not hard to see how the economy bleeds billions of dollars in wasted effort every year while barely noticing.

I use a lot of tech examples to illustrate the importance of decision discipline; however, there are plenty of poor choices across most parts of any business. Operating model choices and talent management are the areas that often turn into a political minefield where the right calls are hard to make, and the wrong ones — while easier in the short term — create much bigger problems down the line.

Wasting Top Talent Through Poor Operating Model Design

A large enterprise employed half a dozen elite data scientists — people who could interrogate terabytes of data and deliver insights within hours. They were the type of talent that could answer almost any business question with speed and rigour.

When a new business line was created, leadership decided to "embed analytics" directly into its operations function. In theory, it sounded reasonable. The business was razor-focused on performance, so the operations function, which was the engine room, felt like a natural "home". In practice, the capability was placed under a leader known for being a "safe pair of hands", valued for process discipline but with little interest or experience in advanced analytics. To this leader, analytics meant having a couple of dashboards to track performance.

One of the corporate data experts was seconded into the unit. Accustomed to solving complex problems, this person found themselves mindlessly scoping and iterating dashboards with vague guidance, little appreciation for the craft, and no connection to the enterprise's deeper analytics capability. Frustration grew, and within months the specialist disengaged and left. The company had inadvertently squandered top talent.

It was like using a five-thousand-dollar DSLR camera to hammer nails: technically possible, but a gross misuse of capability. Top talent needs top-calibre leadership to thrive and operate at full potential. Without it, value is lost and people walk away.

The real failure wasn't a particular individual — it was a poor decision in operating model design and talent management.

Again, it's a seemingly inconsequential matter, but extrapolate it to hundreds of talented staff across various business units. If talent isn't nurtured and developed under the right leaders, it'll leave. The company can continue investing in head-hunting new top talent, and strengthening its Employee Value Proposition through benefits and perks, only to see that talent walk out the door a few months later.

In many industries, some of the most critical decisions are driven by regulatory and legal constraints. Unlike product features or marketing messages, these are not areas where you can afford to "test and learn". Getting them wrong can have devastating consequences — not just in terms of fines and legal liability, but also through reputational damage, loss of customer trust, and erosion of long-term business value.

Leaders often underestimate how a seemingly small choice in wording, positioning, or compliance can fundamentally change the regulatory category in which a business operates.

When Marketing Outran Regulatory Positioning

A health-tech startup developed an AI-powered app that claimed to screen for a range of conditions — from skin lesions to respiratory illness — using nothing more than a smartphone camera and microphone. The technology was promising, attracting attention as a potential category leader.

In recent years, medical regulators have been paying close attention to software that provides clinical-grade health assessments. The startup initially registered the app under the lowest-risk category of medical devices, positioning it as a diagnostic support tool for clinicians. At that classification level, the regulatory burden was manageable: self-assessment, no clinical trials, minimal ongoing compliance.

The problem started when the go-to-market strategy outran the regulatory positioning. Marketing materials aimed at the general public began promoting the app's diagnostic capabilities — the ability to detect serious conditions and recommend action — at consumer-friendly price points. In most Western markets, marketing cancer-screening or diagnostic tools for sexually transmitted infections directly to the public isn't just frowned upon — it's prohibited.

What had been registered as a clinician's aid was now being promoted as a consumer diagnostic tool. It's hard to know from the outside how this extension beyond the registration scope was justified internally. What is clear is that the regulator noticed. The startup's product registration was placed under review and lapsed without renewal. The path forward required reassessment at a higher risk classification — clinical trials, formal evidence requirements, and a much heavier compliance burden.

The mismatch between marketing positioning and regulatory strategy had turned into a major obstacle to expansion and growth.

This case highlights how regulatory blind spots can destroy value. The lesson is simple: in regulated industries, early and deliberate decisions about compliance are not optional. Engaging experts, stress-testing assumptions, and aligning marketing with legal guardrails must happen well before launch... in some cases, it must actually happen before any development work starts!

Some mistakes, like the regulatory compliance failure, can be big and devastating, triggering fines, legal battles, or reputational damage. Others are smaller, harder to spot, and often dismissed as inconsequential. The challenge for leaders is not to dream of a world where bad decisions disappear altogether, but to build a discipline that increases the ratio of good to bad calls. Because every poor decision — whether it's a small oversight or a major regulatory compliance mistake — adds friction. At best, it clogs the system; at worst, it throws in a spanner that can bring the entire machine to a halt.

Now that we've looked at some examples of «bad» decision-making, a word on what «good» decision-making actually means. Regardless of where a company sits on the strategy spectrum, the competitive edge comes from consistently making more good decisions than mediocre ones over time. Notice the word «good» — not «right». The two often get conflated, but they're very different. A «right» decision is one that, in hindsight, produced the best possible outcome. A «good» decision is one made with the right framing, the right people, the right inputs, and the right level of conviction based on what was known at the time.

You can't expect to always make «right» calls. The information is incomplete, the future is uncertain, and even sound reasoning sometimes gets crushed by the imperfections of the real world. Obsessing over perfection is dangerous, particularly when time is of the essence, which is often the case. The 50:1 Method we cover in the rest of this book is all about consistently making good decisions across all levels of the organisation. In aggregate, those good calls will mostly turn out to be right ones, and over time they compound into strong, sustained performance.

Making consistently good decisions starts with knowing which ones actually matter. In the next chapter, we introduce the 50:1 rule and explore why a tiny fraction of decisions drives more than half of your outcomes, and how to focus your energy where it matters most.

Chapter 3:
The 50:1 Rule

"The main thing is to keep the main thing the main thing."

— STEPHEN COVEY

The Better Version of 80:20

I've always felt that the "80:20" principle is overrated. Working 70-hour weeks on intense strategy consulting gigs, I wondered why I was getting smashed despite religiously focusing on the proverbial top 20% of causes that drive 80% of effects. My natural laziness helped me realise that the principle needs a little tweak, which makes it 20x more powerful!

Instead of abstract "causes" and "effects" for simplicity let's think about it as effort (input) vs value (output). If a certain complex problem takes 100 hours to fully solve, by focusing efforts on the highest priority elements of it, in just 20 hours, you should be able to solve 80% of the overall problem.

But here is the trick: the "80:20" rule applies to those 20 hours as well! In fact, by spending only 4 hours (20% of 20 hours), you could tackle 64% (80% of the 80%) of the problem.

That's great, but it doesn't stop there. With the right focus, in under 1 hour (that is 20% of 4 hours), you could smash over half (~51% = 80% of 64%) of the problem! Well, at least in theory. But as we'll see throughout this book this seemingly radical theory is supported by common sense and a lot of evidence from business practice.

FIGURE 3.1: POWER LAW CURVE

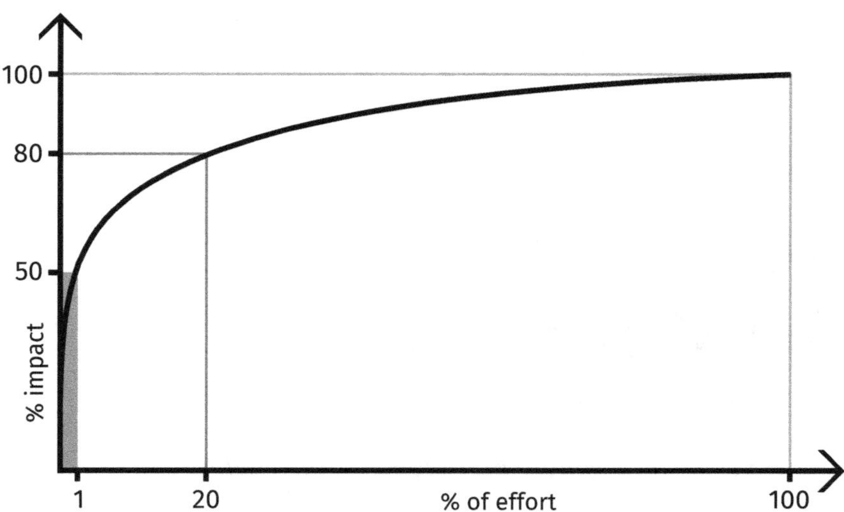

There you have it, 50:1 magic. One hour of prioritised effort yields more than half of the value that working for 100 hours would produce. You may wonder if we could go even further to 1/5 of an hour (0.2% of total effort = 20% of 1%) delivering 41% of the result. Of course, you could, but it's getting hard to argue that solving less than half of the problem is ever going to be good enough.

So, let's stick with 50:1 for now.

A note on terminology. In most business books, "one-percenter" refers to the practice of pursuing many small improvements — each delivering a marginal gain — that compound into significant outcomes over time. In this book, the meaning is almost the opposite. A one-percenter is a decision that disproportionately influences the success or failure of a project, venture, or even the whole business. Getting those one-percenters right takes you halfway to success. Getting those wrong, takes you off track so far that no amount of effort elsewhere will fix it.

Isn't This Just Prioritisation?

A sceptical reader could say "I already prioritise my work. What's the point of this approach?" The distinction is important to understand.

The standard prioritisation is focused on ranking tasks by importance and urgency. If something is important and urgent it gets more attention quicker. This makes sense.

The widely used version of this thinking is the Eisenhower Matrix, a two-by-two grid that orders tasks by urgency and importance. It traces back to a 1954 speech where Dwight Eisenhower, then US president, said that: "I have two kinds of problems, the urgent and the important. The urgent are not important, and the important are never urgent". It's a genuinely useful tool for filtering out noise and making sure important-but-not-urgent work doesn't get perpetually crowded out by whatever is on fire today.

However, the 50:1 approach challenges the conventional two-by-two prioritisation wisdom. The problem is that the "distribution of impact", particularly when it comes to consequential choices, is often so extreme that conventional prioritisation will under-allocate attention to the top. Yes, those critical decisions will sit close to the top of the list, but they will sit alongside many second order choices with high urgency.

Most leaders who think they're good at prioritising would be spreading effort across the top 20% — which is good, but not great. Their priority window is still 20x too wide.

The point of 50:1 is not about working on important things — everyone does that. It's about recognising that one of those important things often matters more than all the others combined and deserves a disproportionate share of leadership attention.

50:1 Is a Law of Nature

This 50:1 principle is a twin of the Price law, which states that the square root of the number of people in a domain produce 50% of the output. In crude business terms, it means that in an organisation with 10,000 staff, the top 100 employees generate half of the value. But please don't mention it in front of your People & Culture colleagues.

It may seem shockingly unfair, but 50:1 is the power law of nature. In many domains, more than half of the output (in value terms) comes from 1% of contributors. 1% of Wikipedia editors generate 77% of the content.

1% of artists earn over 75% of the music industry income. In classical music, only 4 (!) composers (Bach, Beethoven, Mozart and Tchaikovsky) wrote most of the music that is performed by orchestras today. Not surprisingly, this law also applies to how the wealth is distributed: 1% of people hold over 50% of the global net wealth.

Fighting this law may seem noble, but it is akin to fighting gravity. Obviously, it's pointless. But also, why fight if we can use it to our benefit?

The principle can be particularly helpful in delivering change and innovation. Here is a practical interpretation of it: 50% of project success is determined by the 1% of effort (usually early stage including strategy, scoping and design, but not exclusively as we'll uncover in the following chapter).

For example, on a major IT project that involves 1,000 pages of documentation and tens of thousands of lines of code, the most important 10 pages of scope, key design decisions, and requirements will determine 50% of its success.

50:1 Is Not the "Be-All and End-All"

To those of us who get really excited about getting razor-focused and chopping the 99% off their to-do list, here is a word of caution. 50:1 approach does not mean that the remaining 99% is irrelevant. Nor does it mean that execution is unimportant. Like any tool it can be very helpful or cause harm, if used incorrectly.

What it stresses is that the marginal return on leadership or key SME attention is wildly asymmetric, so it pays off to ensure that you nail that critical 1%. However, if you nail the 1% and botch the 99%, you will still fail — that's 100% guaranteed.

The principle should be used to work out where to invest your scarce resource to maximise your chances of success. The resource in this context could be anything from leadership or SME capacity to funding. However, the chances of success won't go up by neglecting everything else. Using our analogy from chapter 1, 50:1 approach tells us to invest time and effort in determining direction with a "compass", but you can't get there without the "engine".

Some may say, "but what if I'm working on the 99% most of the time? Does this concept deem all of my work unimportant?" Not at all — in fact, there is another 1% within the 99% and another one within the next 98%.

Let's take a scenario where a company is launching a new product line. From the CEO's perspective, this may fall squarely in the 99% bucket. The CEO's 1% may gravitate towards capital allocation and consideration of which geographic markets to enter. However, for the Group Executive (GE) responsible for the category and General Manager (GM) responsible for the product line various aspects of this project could fit in their respective 1%. GE may be keen to nail the target segment and investment requirements. GM may need to focus on the key product features and go-to-market. Head of Product will focus on product design and timely delivery. Individual team members will have different 1%-ers depending on their roles, e.g. developing a successful marketing campaign, standing up a dedicated sales website, setting up reliable customer support.

Does the Group Executive need to sweat over the billboard copy? Probably not. However, for the marketing lead a choice of punchy headline could be a make-or-break decision.

As we see in this example, 50:1 approach is not limited to the enterprise level prioritisation, but can exist at any level of the organisation. Regardless of what you do, you need to find your own 1% and nail it every time, because 50% of your personal success hinges on it!

Applying the 50:1 Rule in Business and Life

The 50:1 principle is not just a cute mathematical concept. It can be a powerful operating discipline, which is at the core of the method that is proposed in this book. When applied deliberately, it changes how you allocate time, energy, and resources across everything from project delivery to strategic planning. But it cuts both ways: get the 1% right and you're half-way to success; get it wrong and no amount of effort on the remaining 99% will save you. Here are four things to keep in mind when putting it into practice.

1) **20% of the 1% ain't good enough.** The common pitfall is to drop a "great idea" or high-level strategy (I call it the "0.2%") on

the delivery teams and hope they will sort out the rest. How many projects and transformation programs have gone south due to that "0.8%" strategy-to-execution gap? Whether the company uses in-house capability or external advisors to take the initiative past the critical 1% mark, it must ensure they deliver up to the point where business has enough confidence and can put the pedal to the metal.

2) **Invest disproportionally to get that 1% right.** The hardest part is actually to figure out what that critical 1% is. That is why it is essential to invest the best talent from across the business (and attract externals if required) to ask the right questions and get the best possible answers leveraging available data and expertise. 1% of effort does not have to be equal to 1% of cost. More on this in the following chapters.

3) **1% is not about strategy packs — it's about the critical path.** Sometimes the most important issues and decisions hide in the weeds, that 36,000 feet view of senior leaders will not catch. It's not uncommon to see seemingly trivial downstream decisions dramatically impacting the critical path and leading to costly last-minute remediation. More on this in chapter 9.

4) **Like all rules, it's not without exceptions.** Who would want airline engineers to take shortcuts in making aircraft maintenance decisions or surgeon focusing on quickly addressing half of the symptoms in the operating theatre? Sometimes it has to be 100:100.

The critical path principle above deserves a double-click. We'll get into a lot more detail on the critical path in the next couple of chapters, but it is important to round out the concept while it's front of mind.

If applied to a project, 50:1 approach can be used across all stages, not just at the time of strategy, planning and design. Yes, it is the most impactful when applied at these earlier phases, but it can add lots of value throughout the whole project lifecycle.

In most projects, particularly large-scale ones, the highest-leverage decisions cluster early — during the phase when the strategy gets formulated and designs are getting locked in. However, consequential choices can happen at any stage. In the descoping disaster example, when a two-week "time-saving" tweak nearly triggered operational havoc. The decision was made hastily at a Steering Committee meeting, probably alongside many other business-as-usual discussion topics. They just saw it as a bottom-of-the-99% issue, but it turned out to be a true one-percenter.

The early 1% can include choices around strategic direction, architecture, vendor selection, operating model, team structure. The mid-flight 1% could involve scope pivots, design and feature adjustments, integration decisions, change management. The late 1% may cover launch readiness, staff training, go/no-go milestones, contingency plans, rollback criteria, and so on.

The upshot is that we can't drop the guard after the strategy phase is completed. Disciplined 50:1 practitioners at any level need to stay alert for new 1% choices emerging throughout delivery and even post-launch.

The Fittings That Nearly Sank the Contract

An engineering company was installing a fire suppression system in one of the largest office developments in Central Asia. At the final stage of the project, a supplier failed to deliver a batch of metal fittings. Without them, the entire installation came to a complete halt as the deadline rapidly approached and penalties loomed.

The procurement team tried to source the fittings domestically. Nothing was available. They put out a call to the offices in other countries. Two came back. The first could source the fittings and deliver them by truck within a week. The second had them available immediately, but they would need to be air-freighted, with a two-day turnaround. The catch was that airfreight would essentially double the cost.

Neither of the options felt clean and the divisional director was going to take a day to think it through and explore other alternatives. The CEO overheard the conversation. His response was instant: "The penalty for delay on this contract is over a hundred times higher than the cost of airfreight. We don't have time to think — ship it now".

The fittings arrived two days later. The installation resumed. The contract stayed on track.

The divisional director was trying to be responsible with the budget. But he was working in a "19%" or "80%" decision mode. While the CEO immediately realised that the massive contract penalty risk made it a "1%" deal-breaker that needed to be resolved immediately.

50:1 Rule in Decision-Making

While it's great to know that good decision-making takes us half-way to success, too often we jump to "making the right decision" without first thinking "which decision" we must get right. In business and in everyday life, we face hundreds of choices varying in importance and complexity. It's best to start by figuring out where to focus efforts.

To some, the 50:1 concept may have felt a bit theoretical so far, now we are getting the crunchy part. Let's now apply the approach to decision-making. On a beautiful pareto curve we can distinguish three tiers of decisions:

1) **Die in the ditch for.** This is the critical 1% that you must nail. Often, there are a few fundamental choices that set direction. These strategic hard-to-reverse decisions can range from go-to-market (e.g. which product to develop) to back-of-house (e.g. which core IT platform to select).

2) **Get it right.** These are the following 19% that also matter. Once the direction is set, the second layer of decisions can either keep you on track if "right" or take you off-piste if botched. These are enduring choices (e.g. which product features to add or which software to customise vs use out of the box) and deserve some effort.

3) **Don't stuff up.** That's the remaining 80% of the issues that won't move the needle. Using our definition from chapter 1 these probably don't even qualify for "decision" as inconsequential. Nonetheless, they shouldn't be neglected, but receive just enough effort not to stuff those up and to stay out of trouble — where possible delegate, pick default, automate.

A lot in this book is focused on the 1%, but let's look at the 80% for a minute. The 80% of decisions that won't move the needle are precisely the sorts of task that AI tools can help chew through at lightning-fast speed. Summarising reports, triaging requests, drafting standard responses, running quick-and-dirty analysis on routine questions. If you set them up right, AI tools can take out a meaningful chunk of that 80%-related effort and radically accelerate your path to decision. That's a good thing, particularly if leaders redirect the freed-up bandwidth to what actually matters. The risk I foresee is the opposite, where leaders generate more analysis on everything, drown in options and insights, and stall decision-making. Let's not allow that to happen.

Everyone across an organisation at their respective level will have their own "1%", "19%", and "80%" issues. The effectiveness of leaders to a significant extent depends on their ability to focus their personal and team's energy on nailing the most consequential issues.

FIGURE 3.2: POWER LAW IN DECISION-MAKING

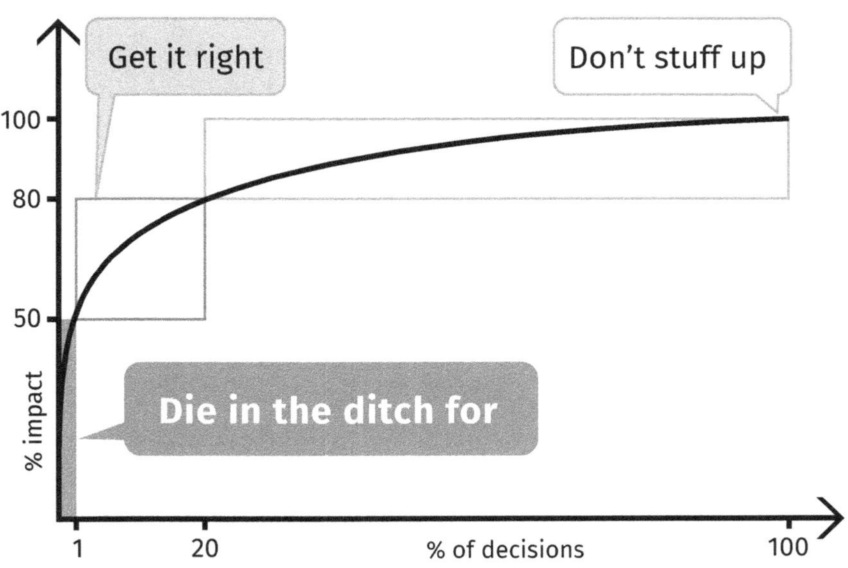

How an Issue Can Be 1%, 19% and 80% at the Same Time

When a major insurer was scaling its wellbeing rewards program one of the simplest — yet most impactful — innovations came directly from the team. It was identified, designed, and implemented entirely by the team for whom it mattered — without any leadership involvement.

The issue was subtle but costly. To prevent abuse, the program implemented an annual cap on the points that customers could earn for healthy actions like steps, exercise, and sleep. In the fourth quarter of the year, some of the most engaged customers began hitting the cap. When their points for completed challenges and goals stopped showing up in the transaction history, confusion followed — hundreds of phone calls and emails flooded in every month.

From the perspective of a Group Executive who is managing a multi-billion-dollar business, a few hundred extra emails and calls are a rounding error — the bottom of "80%" bucket matter. For the General Manager overseeing the program, it's a "19%" issue that's not a deal breaker, but material enough to keep an eye on. For the operations team, however, this was clearly a "1% to die for" — one of the top three customer issues responsible for a substantial share of enquiries.

The operations team set out to find a pragmatic solution. They explored multiple options: from triggered comms campaigns and in-app notifications, to program rules and system changes. But one idea stood out: issue a single point with the short description "Annual points cap reached". This way, customers checking their transaction history would instantly see and understand why their rewards had stopped, without needing to call or email.

The solution was elegant and near costless. The decision to implement was swift. For just one cent per maxed-out customer and a simple automated script, the problem was tackled literally overnight and for good. For the senior leadership, it was an example of excellent execution; for the operations team, it was a hallmark of effective decision-making.

Leaders must be very deliberate on how they invest their time and energy. Their attention, which is a scarce resource, needs to span multiple domains from content and problem-solving to people and performance management, thought leadership, stakeholder engagement, and admin. A substantial share of the time that the leaders spend in the content and problem-solving domain should be dedicated to the 1%. As a rule of thumb, the "get it right 19%" can be delegated to the direct reports. In most cases, the leader's 19%-ers will be their 1%-ers. The bottom 80% can be delegated further or tackled quickly – e.g. through System 1 (fast) thinking relying on gut feel and experience.

The watchout in the problem classification is to ensure that you don't overlook any one-percenters in the 19% and 80% buckets. We'll unpack how to do it in more detail in the subsequent chapters, but it's important to touch on it in this context to fully bring it to life. Sometimes a highly consequential decision doesn't appear material. It can be buried in technical detail, legal fine print, or dry operational process.

The black-belt level decision-making skill isn't about prioritising the obvious big calls. Rather, it's about developing the instinct to recognise when something in the weeds is on the critical path. What distinguishes leaders and SMEs who catch these hidden 1% decisions from those who don't? Three key things are worth highlighting: pattern recognition that gets honed through experience, genuine curiosity and comfort to go into fine detail when it matters, and thinking few steps ahead by asking "What breaks if we get this wrong?" at every level — not just in the boardroom.

When Cost Optimisation Becomes the Most Expensive Decision

A subscription-based business engaged consultants to improve efficiency and optimise costs. The team identified a dozen opportunities and allocated comparable effort to planning and implementing each of those — financial analysis, implementation planning, business case sign-off, change management and delivery.

Among those opportunities was a recommendation to disconnect an expensive payment option and migrate customers to cheaper alternatives. A couple of million dollars of projected annual savings were comparable to the other initiatives in the spreadsheet.

What wasn't in the spreadsheet was that this payment option was preferred by a significant share of loyal, long-term customers. When forced to switch, tens of thousands encountered friction. Because of the subscription model, the impact hit hard at renewal time — frustrated customers chose not to update their payment details and to leave instead. The revenue lost from departing customers was an order of magnitude higher than the savings.

Of the portfolio of cost-out initiatives, majority were genuine 80-percenters — routine optimisations, removal of functional duplication, and frontline efficiency. One was a 1%-er in disguise: a decision that directly touched a critical aspect of customer experience and consequently retention. The team applied 80% rigour to a problem that demanded 1% scrutiny and the business paid dearly.

One more thing on the 1%. Finding the right answer matters, but finding it at the right speed matters just as much. Colin Powell's rule of thumb is to never decide with less than 40% of the information you need, but never wait for more than 70%. Beyond that, the cost of delay almost always exceeds the value of additional data. We come back to the discipline of pace in Chapter 7.

While this all may sound like common sense, the challenge is in identifying and articulating that 1%. It takes a lot of practice, experience, and intellectual "horsepower". Just finding and facing those "die in the ditch for" issues puts Kahneman's System 2 (slow) thinking in overdrive. Let's explore this in more detail in chapters 4 and 5.

Chapter 4:
The "1% To Die For"

"The most serious mistakes are not being made as a result of wrong answers. The truly dangerous thing is asking the wrong question."

— PETER DRUCKER

In chapter 3 we introduced the 50:1 rule — the idea that leaders need to focus their efforts on the most consequential issues, where the top 1% makes a comparable contribution to the overall success as the remaining 99%. Call it hyperfocused decision-making: the discipline of concentrating leadership and team attention and rigour where it delivers extraordinary leverage, rather than spreading it thinly across everything that comes your way.

Some issues deserve hours of debate and rigour. Others should be made in minutes or delegated entirely. The art of decision-making lies in spotting and nailing that 1%. This chapter will unpack the first step — how to identify the "1% of decisions to die for".

The Pyramid of Decision-Making

Finding this crucial 1% to focus on is far from trivial. Game-changing and show-stopping choices can arise at any level: from the "sexy" strategy to the seemingly "boring" execution, from a 36,000-ft decision on which markets to enter to a dry privacy policy clause.

This 1% doesn't have to be "big". Sometimes, perfecting five words of a promo headline requires more effort than a 200-page industry report.

As our careers progress, we often get stuck at the top of the pyramid, but successful leaders must not neglect critical design, delivery, and operational issues. An overlooked test case can derail a massive project. An underestimated campaign uptake can blow up operations and ruin customer experience. A revised interpretation of a regulation clause can deem the whole strategy obsolete.

An issue at the bottom of the pyramid may require significant changes at the top, and vice versa.

Nail the strategy, then put your blood, sweat and tears to work through the details that are a matter of life or death for the project — the 1%. For the remaining "99%" — leaders should step aside and let the team make the magic happen.

But we've already seen that the 1% concept is not exclusive to leaders! Each team member needs to find and crack their 1% first... before working out the rest.

Think of decision-making as a pyramid.

At the very top are a few big, strategic calls: acquisitions, market entries, new products, capital allocation shifts. These are obviously important. What's crucial here is ensuring that the decisions are aligned with enterprise objectives and equally important with each other. It's not uncommon to see organisations setting ambitious targets for the high-potential business line and then suffocating it by diverting resources to salvage "underperformers".

At the very bottom are thousands of daily execution decisions: scheduling, copy, formatting, frontline training, regulatory compliance, process tweaks. In most cases, they're routine, low-impact, and best left to delivery teams. However, given the sheer volume of those, it's not uncommon to come across a few landmines there. Many of us have experienced firsthand a minor operational issue wreaking havoc in a large-scale enterprise project. I've seen cases where a minor inconsistency in the way the analytics tagging was applied in an app nearly derailed a multi-million-dollar campaign that was reliant upon that tagging.

In the middle are the real minefields — choices that may look small in the moment but carry hidden leverage. A seemingly small call on design or scope may result in having to rebuild a big chunk of the solution down the track, when it becomes apparent that the feature was implemented too narrowly. A single clause in a regulation, five words in a marketing headline, a tweak to how an algorithm works — any of these can tip the balance between success and failure. The real art is finding that 1% needle in the haystack.

FIGURE 4.1: DECISION-MAKING PYRAMID

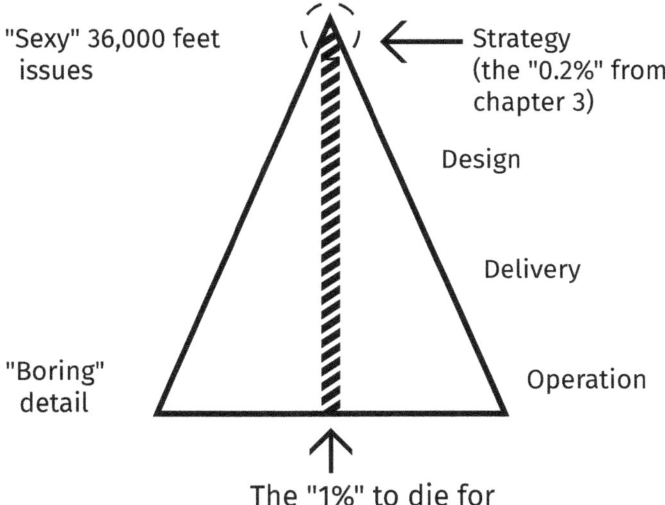

Two Dimensions of the 1%

So how do you know which decisions belong to that 1%? You need a lens. There are two dimensions you need to be on the lookout for: reversibility and criticality. Reversibility is exactly what it says on the tin. It's all about the flexibility to pivot or reverse the choice. Criticality is about the likely magnitude of impact on success or failure. Taken together, these help you locate the "1% frontier" — the imaginary border between the 1% and the rest.

Let's look at these two dimensions in a bit more detail.

One-Way vs Two-Way Doors

Amazon popularised the idea of "one-way" and "two-way" doors. It's a simple but powerful frame.

Two-way doors are reversible. You can walk through, try something, and if it doesn't work, step back. Examples: experimenting with a website layout, trialling a small pilot, tweaking an internal policy. These decisions are relatively cheap to reverse.

One-way doors are irreversible or very costly and time-consuming to undo. Once you step through, there's no easy way back. Examples: choosing a core technology platform, entering a regulated market, signing a long-term supply agreement.

A One-Way Door That Was Missed

A major bank developed a comprehensive rewards program for its customers. As part of it they implemented a state-of-the-art Loyalty Management Platform (LMS). LMS is essentially the general ledger of a program that tracks all the points earned and redeemed.

A year into the program, as a result of significant customisation and complexity of managing this custom code base, the LMS was "forked". It means that the program ended up on the "frozen" version of the platform that was not evolving in line with the core cloud-based platform, but was only tweaked to accommodate specific change requests.

There was no explicit decision about it — at least not that anyone can recall. It was probably mentioned casually at one of the monthly Steering Committee meetings. Nobody paid attention until two years later, when the bank needed a set of features, which turned out to be unavailable on the forked version.

No one realised it was a one-way door situation. If anybody sounded the alarm around the time the fork happened, the team would have opted in for a few months' delay in delivery to remain focused on the core code base.

Due to this unfortunate miss, it took two years and a large-scale project to migrate back to the core code base!

Obviously, one-way doors require a lot more care and attention; however, it's not uncommon to see leaders doing the opposite. They escalate trivial reversible choices, burning time and energy debating options that could have been tried and validated in a matter of days. Worse, some sleepwalk through into long-term commitments, treating irrevocable decisions with casualness and ignorance.

The first question when facing a decision should be: If we get this wrong, how hard is it to unwind?

Criticality to Success or Failure

The second dimension is criticality. Not every irreversible decision matters. Not every reversible one is trivial. The real question is: Does this decision sit on the fault line of success or failure?

High-criticality decisions directly and/or dramatically impact outcomes. If you get them wrong, the strategy fails. Example: determining features of the new product, designing a loyalty program's earn model, or choosing a technology platform for the new service line.

Low-criticality decisions have limited bearing on overall success. Example: the colour of office chairs, the choice of service email templates — the ones that no one reads (albeit, in some cases, even this can be critical), the brand of coffee in the boardroom (although some Melbournians would violently disagree on that one).

The trap here is misjudging importance. Some leaders obsess over visible, symbolic issues (logos, PowerPoint templates, news mentions) while overlooking "boring stuff": back-end system limitations, regulatory constraints, or vendor dependencies that can make or break the project or even the entire business.

When it comes to critical issues, two special types are worth keeping top of mind. I call them "show-stoppers" and "game-changers".

A show-stopper can be something big or small that, if not dealt with, can derail the entire project. A good example of a show-stopper in action is the Descoping Disaster case study from chapter 1. The project team decided to save some development effort by descoping one of the most critical algorithms (without realising it). This seemingly small omission could have been catastrophic for business operations.

A game-changer is the opposite of a show-stopper. It's something that could dramatically improve the outcomes or chances of success. Say you are running a successful national rewards program and an opportunity comes up to bring on board a new partner that could add 20% of points turnover to the program. That's a game-changer. All key decisions associated with it become critical and deserve extreme care.

The Painful Game-Changer

Two years after the launch of a rewards program as a standalone app, a financial services major realised that the business was running out of early adopters — those willing to download a rewards app and engage with the company across two digital platforms. Weekly sign-ups started to slow, despite increasingly generous rewards, and active promotional activity.

The scale-up squad threw everything at the problem — new campaigns, richer incentives, and countless experiments — but the growth trajectory barely budged. It was clear that to keep growing, the program needed to pivot and integrate into the main app, which at the time had an order of magnitude more users.

Even suggesting such a move felt taboo. The idea of an agile new venture merging into the "mothership" app raised real fears: loss of momentum, extra bureaucracy, added complexity, and the risk of destabilising a critical core platform. How would hundreds of thousands of loyal rewards users be transitioned from a standalone app? Would brand identity and retention suffer?

The decision wasn't easy. Integration also meant wiping out 12–18 months of the planned innovation pipeline. Many features on the development roadmap would have to be delayed or cancelled. But with growth slowing down, those future features could become meaningless. The business case was unambiguous: without a larger user base, all that innovation wouldn't be commercially viable in the long run.

The integration into the core app was clearly a game-changer. It was expected to reignite growth, simplify the user experience, and boost engagement and retention. The decision to integrate was one of the most difficult and consequential in the program's history.

It took a lot of careful analysis and planning, but in the end, it delivered exactly what was expected. The business saw a step change in growth and engagement performance at a larger scale, which in turn ensured the program's long-term sustainability and positive impact on customer retention.

The 1% Frontier

If we put the two dimensions together, we get a "two-by-two". Well, kind of. These dimensions are not binary. They should be viewed as spectrums of reversibility and criticality. When either of the dimensions is very high or both are relatively high, it's a good indicator that you're facing a one-percenter that deserves attention.

FIGURE 4.2: THE 1% FRONTIER

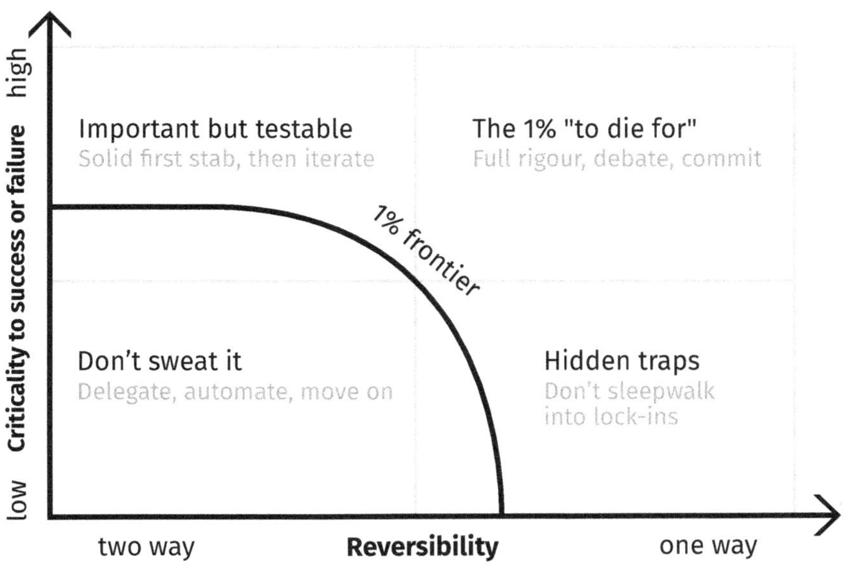

If we followed the Economics 101 approach to decision-making, we would call it a "1% frontier". A curve that separates what's critical from what's not. To state the obvious, the one-percenters are on the outer side of the frontier. What lands on the inner side is less important.

In broad terms, if we mentally split this matrix into four quadrants, we'd treat choices sitting across those quadrants differently.

Critical + One-Way Door: These are the true one-percenters to die for. They deserve the full weight of rigour, debate, and escalation if required. Before you commit, you need to be confident that the right call is made.

Critical + Two-Way Door: Important, but testable. The common approach here is to have a solid first stab at the problem, but then to run experiments and iterate. Given the criticality, it can't be a "quick and dirty" approach, but you wouldn't spend months perfecting the decision before committing. An example could be selecting a service provider for a critical capability, where the switching costs are relatively affordable. A property management company that is running a portfolio of Airbnbs is absolutely critical to business success, but the landlord can switch to another provider with a month's notice if things don't go to plan.

Non-Critical + One-Way Door: Hidden traps. They look peripheral but can lock you in. These need visibility to avoid accidental cost sinks. There are plenty of examples in the corporate world of what I call "a suitcase without a handle" — burdensome, yet too costly or uncomfortable to abandon. Products, services or partnerships that linger there in the lights-on mode, consuming a little bit of effort and resources, just because it would take a lot of effort and resources to shut those down.

Non-Critical + Two-Way Door: Don't sweat those. Delegate, automate, or decide quickly. That's not 1%.

The two-by-two gives you a good lens for an individual decision. But in practice, decisions don't sit in isolation — they cascade. A strategic choice at the top of the pyramid reshapes what's critical at the design level, which in turn redefines the options at the execution level. The frontier isn't static; it shifts as you move through the layers of the organisation. So, the next question is: what happens when decisions have upstream or downstream impacts?

Up and Down the Pyramid

If finding the 1% in the pyramid isn't hard enough, applying it requires looking both upstream and downstream — understanding how a single decision can ripple across strategy, design, execution, and even day-to-day operations. Nailing that 1% often demands moving up and down the pyramid iteratively, testing how choices at one level affect the others. Let's look at an example.

Imagine a health company planning to launch a telehealth service. The objective that teams are tasked with is to expand customer engagement in preventive health, at scale.

The initial plan could be to offer one free trial consultation and charge standard market rates for any follow-up or subsequent consultations. This "try before you buy" model would lower barriers for customers and help build trust in the service.

As the product team progresses, however, a potential regulatory "show-stopper" may emerge. For instance, a free health consultation might be considered a high-risk service depending on the interpretation of certain health services regulations. If that turned out to be the case, every consultation would have to be billed at market rates. Suddenly, the entire growth model would be at risk. Without an introductory free offer, customer uptake would slow dramatically. With fewer bookings, clinician utilisation would drop, driving inefficiencies and higher per-session costs. What started as a design challenge in the middle of the pyramid could jeopardise both operational viability (at the base of the pyramid) and the strategic growth objective (at the top).

The alignment across people or functions working on the 1% is essential. When teams collaborate closely — product, legal, operations, finance — they can identify these dependencies early and pivot together. But when teams operate in silos, even small adjustments can push a large project off track.

Picture the product team quietly removing the free consultation offer after a legal red flag, adjusting their marketing materials and take-up accordingly, while operations continue hiring clinicians to meet the original, now unrealistic, demand forecasts. Finance might still be budgeting for free consultations that will never happen. The result: chaos, rework, and wasted investment.

Now, imagine the opposite scenario — where the regulatory issue is solved and the product team has found capacity to fund a couple of "free" consultations each year as a benefit of the subscription product that most of its customer base holds. That one change could be transformative. Offering a couple of free sessions per year would not only dramatically increase uptake, but build a usage habit, which will subsequently drive usage of paid sessions after the free ones get used up. Ultimately, it could become an accelerated path to a self-reinforcing flywheel of growth and engagement. That's how a decision to improve a proposition (in the middle of the pyramid) unlocks operational efficiency (at the bottom) and brings forward long-term strategic objectives (at the top).

FIGURE 4.3: DECISION-MAKING PYRAMID IN ACTION

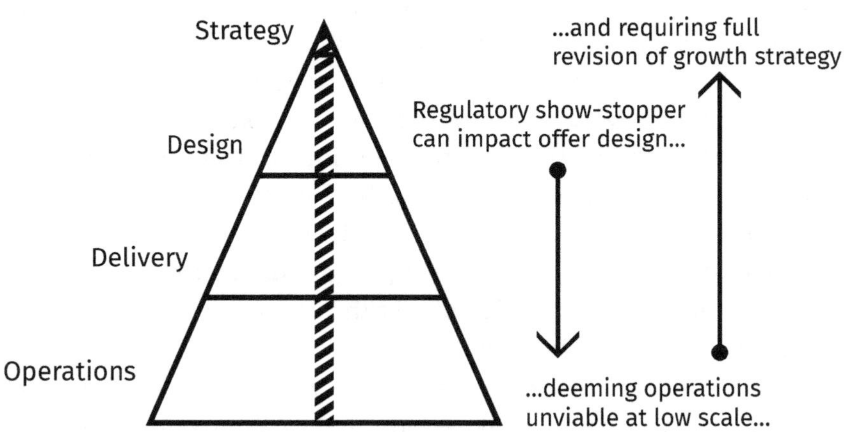

As we've seen in the hypothetical example above, when dealing with the 1% that matters, we can't analyse choices in isolation. When you change one element — free consultations, in this case — trace its downstream impacts (i.e. can operations handle the consequences?) and upstream implications (i.e. does this threaten the strategy?). Often, the successes and failures of the most consequential choices are determined in those interconnections.

A disciplined, iterative approach up and down the pyramid is how leaders avoid costly mistakes and achieve lasting outcomes.

Getting It Right

A big part of leadership is not about making all the decisions, but about correctly classifying which decisions to focus scarce attention on, and which ones to "short circuit" or delegate.

If the framework is so simple, why do so many miss the 1%? Multiple reasons. Some are overconfident in reversibility. Leaders assume they can try now and pivot later. They may underestimate sunk costs, contractual lock-ins, and cultural inertia that make reversals difficult and/or costly. Some misjudge criticality. It's easier to obsess over visible choices than hidden ones. Executives may debate branding endlessly, but wave through complex system architectures with little scrutiny. Some leaders may avoid one-percenters to avoid conflict, when the call may require escalation, debate, and accountability. It's easier to pretend it's an operational call and hope for the better.

How can leaders avoid these traps? A few practical approaches:

— Ask "Is this reversible?" and "Is this critical?" out loud. Make those two questions part of every decision framing.
— Map top-of-mind decisions on the two-by-two. Even a rough sketch clarifies where attention is needed. Validate it with the team and key stakeholders.
— Clarify the 1%. Explicitly call out and describe which decisions are "to die for". This signals the team to invest time and effort.
— Default to delegation on the 99%. Free leadership bandwidth by deliberately pushing less critical, reversible calls to the people closest to the execution.

T&Cs Blow Up

A major travel insurer launched a campaign offering loyalty points for buying travel cover. The creative was punchy, and the points headline did exactly what it was meant to do — grab attention.

Buried in the campaign T&Cs was a small omission. The terms didn't require the trip to be taken (or even to commence) before bonus points were credited. At the same time, standard product settings allowed a cancellation with a full refund if no travel had begun and no claim was made.

Online loyalty communities spotted the loophole within hours. A simple playbook spread in forums and group chats. (1) buy the cheapest eligible travel policy for a far-future date, (2) receive the bonus points soon after purchase, (3) cancel after the points landed — refund secured, points kept.

Sales skyrocketed, but so did the queues for policy cancellations. Within days, the campaign was pulled. But the damage was so material that the company had to implement an Interactive Voice Response (IVR) pathway to allow self-service cancellations (i.e. "Press 9 to cancel your travel cover") to get their overflowing contact centre under control.

T&Cs often look like "execution detail". They're not. Campaign terms and points issuance rules are the program's risk surface. In ambiguous, high-velocity campaigns, treat T&Cs as part of the decision, not the admin that follows it.

Closing Challenge

The "1% to die for" choices are never labelled, and are often far from obvious. They don't show up neatly in your board papers or your project dashboards. They hide across various layers of the pyramid, in choices that feel mundane and operational until they explode in your face.

Developing the discipline to spot them is one of the leader's key jobs. And when that 1% is spotted, it must be treated with the seriousness it deserves. Because in the end, it's not the hundreds of routine decisions that define your trajectory. It's the handful that are irreversible, business-critical, and often invisible until it's too late.

This book is about making those decisions consciously — the "1% to die for".

Chapter 5:
The Method of Nailing the 1%

"If I had an hour to solve a problem I'd spend 55 minutes thinking about the problem and five minutes thinking about solutions."

— ALBERT EINSTEIN

Now that you can spot the 1%, the next question is how to consistently nail those decisions once you've identified them.

While there's a degree of decision-making in every role across an organisation — from the CEO to the ball kids at the Australian Open — by now it should be obvious that the focus of this book is on the choices that are the most important. Because the stakes are high, these important choices require robust discipline and a comprehensive, well-structured approach.

The following three chapters introduce the method built around the first three elements of the toolkit: the "Who" (getting the right people and teams involved), the "How" (setting the right culture and operating environment), and the "Why" (ensuring the right framing — objectives, constraints, and questions that define the decision). These three set the stage. Then the fourth element (the analytical process) is covered in the "What" chapter. It provides a step-by-step approach to finding the best answer. Finally, the "Decisions in Complex Systems" chapter offers a practical way to structure and resolve complex, interdependent choices.

But before we roll up our sleeves, it's worth addressing two things: where this method sits relative to other frameworks you may have encountered, and what it is (and isn't) designed to do.

The Landscape of Decision-Making Frameworks

There is no shortage of frameworks that aim to improve organisational decision-making. If you've spent any time in management consulting or large corporates, you've likely come across a few.

RAPID, developed by Bain & Company, assigns clear decision roles: Recommend, Agree, Perform, Input, Decide. It's a useful tool for answering who plays what role in a specific decision. Its strength is creating clarity on accountability. Its limitation is scope. RAPID tells you who's in the room and what their job is. It doesn't help you figure out what questions to ask, which options to consider, or how to evaluate trade-offs. If RAPID is the org chart of a decision, our method is the comprehensive playbook.

RACI (Responsible, Accountable, Consulted, Informed) and its many variants (such as DACI and RASCI) started as a project management tool for task ownership. It's widely understood and simple to apply. But it was never designed for complex strategic choices. It tells you who does what. It doesn't tell you what to do. RACI is fine as a responsibility allocation tool, not a decision-making method.

OODA Loop (Observe, Orient, Decide, Act) was developed by military strategist John Boyd for fast-cycling decisions in dynamic, adversarial environments. It's excellent where speed matters more than depth: battlefield tactics, competitive responses, crisis management. But for multi-faceted strategic decisions where you need to align stakeholders, evaluate complex trade-offs, and commit to a path that's hard to reverse, OODA is too lean. It works well for fighter pilots, but is not ideal for designing new product lines or for entering new markets.

Cynefin Framework, created by Dave Snowden, helps leaders categorise problems into domains: Clear, Complicated, Complex, Chaotic. Each domain calls for a different approach. It's a powerful diagnostic. If you're unsure whether to apply best practice, good practice, or emergent practice, Cynefin helps you figure that out. What it doesn't do is give you the tools once you've made the diagnosis.

Vroom-Yetton Model provides a decision tree for determining how much team involvement a decision requires — from autocratic to fully collaborative. It is useful for calibrating participation, but is narrow. It addresses one dimension (who gets a say) of a much broader challenge.

What most of these frameworks have in common is that they solve for a slice of the puzzle. Role clarity, problem classification, participation level, speed. All those elements are valuable, however, in isolation they are not comprehensive. What's missing is a method that stitches these pieces together: the right team, the right environment, the right problem definition, and the analytical discipline to crack it.

The existing frameworks may work for certain problems or challenges, but are not particularly helpful for the more complex ones. Relying on a methodology like that in a complex decision-making environment is a bit like trying to build a house with a limited set of tools. While a hammer and screwdriver will do multiple jobs at the construction site, it's going to be incredibly challenging to finish the whole job without a full builder's toolbox.

That's what the Who, How, Why, and What method aims to provide. It doesn't replace these frameworks. Elements like RAPID's role clarity or Cynefin's problem categorisation can complement it nicely. But it operates at a broader level, stitching together what other frameworks leave separate. It offers a comprehensive decision-making set of tools that can be applied to nearly any organisational challenge.

What This Method Is (and Isn't)

As we have just touched on, at its core, the 50:1 Method is a comprehensive toolkit for making the critical decisions that disproportionately determine success. It covers the full arc:

— The "Who" (chapter 6): selecting and assembling the right people with the right mindset, capability and expertise.

— The "How" (chapter 7): creating the right cultural conditions through Focus, Openness, Clarity, and Speed that enable quality decisions and honest debate.

— The "Why" (chapter 8): defining objectives, key results, constraints, guiding principles, and importantly starting with the right questions. Making sure you're addressing the right problem before you even start solving it.

— The "What" (chapter 9): the analytical process — generating options, evaluating trade-offs, making recommendations, debating, committing, and executing.

You may wonder how come "Who" and "How" chapters are before "Why". After all, in most situations you could start by defining the problem and objectives before assembling the team to crack it. That's a perfectly valid approach, and if you'd prefer to jump to chapter 8 first, go for it. The sequencing in this book is deliberate, though. The approaches we discuss in "Who" and "How" chapters are foundational and enduring. The right people, mindset, and culture will serve you across dozens of decisions, projects, and strategy cycles. They are not hard-wired to a single problem. The "Why" and the "What", on the other hand, are typically applied fresh each time a new consequential decision lands on your desk. Build the foundation once, use it many times.

The method is designed to tackle the most complex, multi-faceted strategic decisions. The kind where the stakes are high, the options are ambiguous, multiple stakeholders are involved, and the consequences are hard to reverse. These are the one-percenters from chapter 3 — the choices that deserve a disproportionate share of leadership attention and effort.

That said, it scales down. Many of the individual tools apply to more tactical decisions too. Back to our construction example, when building a house from the ground up, you need many tools, various equipment and construction materials. To replace a showerhead, a spanner should be sufficient. The following chapters provide the full toolkit. However, not every decision will require every tool. Having these tools at your disposal and being able to utilise them effectively is what matters.

Those with a management consulting background will recall methodologies like the hypothesis-driven approach (HDA), pyramid principle, mutually exclusive collectively exhaustive (MECE) structuring, and deductive and inductive problem-solving. These are all powerful analytical techniques. They complement this method really well, particularly in the Analysis section of the "What" (chapter 9). Think of the 50:1 Method as operating at a level above those methodologies. It provides the strategic framing — objectives, constraints, questions, options — within which HDA and the pyramid principle do their best work. Without that framing, even brilliant analysis risks solving the wrong problem. The customer trust case study in chapter 8 is a vivid example of exactly that.

One more thing. The real world doesn't always present decisions as neat, standalone choices. Sometimes you face a web of interdependent decisions where everything affects everything else — what I call projects with infinite degrees of freedom. Chapter 9 provides the method for individual decisions. Chapter 10 extends it to those ultra-complex environments and shows how to navigate decision webs without losing your mind. It also illustrates a practical cut-through approach to an often-painful enterprise decisioning process — capital budgeting.

AI tools can now compress weeks of analysis into hours, helping teams generate options, model scenarios, synthesise data. But this acceleration only helps if your people can make decisions at matching speed: if they have clarity on objectives, can debate openly, and can commit with conviction. Without that discipline, AI just produces faster analysis of unclear questions.

Now, let's get into it. We start with the foundation: the "who" and the "how". Because no process, however rigorous, can compensate for not having the right people in the room, or a culture that rewards optics and punishes honesty.

Part Two

The Toolkit

Chapter 6:
The "Who"

"First who, then what. Get the right people on the bus, the wrong people off the bus, and the right people in the right seats."

— JIM COLLINS

However good a method is, it won't survive contact with the wrong team. You can have the sharpest analytical process, the clearest objectives, and a culture that rewards honesty, but if the people involved in making the call lack the right mindset and capability, the output will be mediocre at best.

This chapter unpacks what to look for in the individuals and teams that the organisation entrusts with its most consequential decisions. We'll start with the profile of a good decision-maker, then explore how to assemble teams that consistently deliver under pressure and ambiguity.

Profile of a Good Decision-Maker

If there was a number one prerequisite to being a good decision-maker, it would be the willingness to take responsibility. Unless someone is ready to own outcomes completely, take accountability when things go wrong, and give credit to others when they go right, delegating serious decisions to them is risky.

In the language of leadership, this is extreme ownership. The term was popularised by Jocko Willink and Leif Babin, former U.S. Navy SEALs, in their 2015 book Extreme Ownership: How U.S. Navy SEALs Lead and

Win. If you haven't seen Jocko's Extreme Ownership TED talk — make sure you look it up on YouTube. That's 13 minutes of raw leadership inspiration seen by close to 9 million people.

Their simple but powerful idea is that leaders must own everything in their area. There's no one else to blame. If the team fails, it's the leader's fault. If the mission succeeds, it's because the leader created the conditions for success and empowered others to operate at their full potential.

Extreme ownership doesn't mean micromanaging or doing everyone's job. It's about taking full responsibility for outcomes — even when the variables are outside your control. When a leader thinks this way, excuses disappear and problems turn into hurdles that need to be overcome. Decisions become deliberate acts of leadership rather than ad-hoc reactions to circumstances.

But ownership alone isn't enough. Many leaders who take accountability fall short because they're too focused on having things under control and not enough on the progress. The best decision-makers combine extreme ownership with a proactive drive to make things better — to move the organisation forward, not just keep it safe. They don't wait to be told what's wrong; they're already looking for ways to improve. In corporate terms, they're not "a safe pair of hands"; they're catalysts for change.

But before we dive into the matrix, here's an important caveat. The four archetypes that follow describe behaviours, not people. I'm a strong believer that mindset and capability are developed, not fixed. The same person can show up as a "safe pair of hands" in one context and "make magic happen" in another — depending on the stakes, the team around them, the clarity of the mandate, and where they are in their own development arc.

The point of the framework isn't to label colleagues and slot them into boxes. It's to give leaders — and individuals reflecting on their own practice — a vocabulary for spotting which behaviours help good decision-making and which get in the way. Most of us have been in all four quadrants at different points in our careers. The goal is to spend more time in the top-right, and to help others do the same.

This balance between ownership and proactiveness forms a neat two-by-two matrix:

FIFURE 6.1: BEHAVIORAL ARCHETYPES OF DECISION-MAKERS

	Low Proactivity	High Proactivity
High Ownership	✔ Safe pairs of hands – dependable, reliable, deliver what's asked, but rarely push boundaries.	👍 Make magic happen – rare leaders who take full accountability and proactively create positive change.
Low Ownership	⚠ Passengers – drift with the current, avoid accountability, and rarely drive impact.	⚠ Wheel spinners – always busy, full of ideas and motion, but lack follow-through or responsibility.

Let's explore these briefly.

In **passenger mode**, people avoid both responsibility and initiative. They need constant direction and are content staying in their lane. Established organisations tolerate them because they're not overtly disruptive, but they require a lot of oversight and guidance, which drains energy and momentum. When team members slip into passenger mode, leaders often have to shift into micro-management and their colleagues have to pick up the slack.

The wheel-spinning archetype brims with ideas and enthusiasm but lacks discipline and interest in taking responsibility. They chase new shiny objects, volunteer for everything, and deliver little that endures. Their energy can be contagious — until people around them realise that it is not connected to any results. The wheel-spinning archetype is arguably the most problematic of the four — not only do they keep themselves busy with "stuff", but they often create busywork for others.

The safe pairs of hands archetype is every leader's comfort zone. They take ownership and keep things moving along, protecting the business from surprises. They're indispensable for business continuity but rarely initiate step-change. Without heavy top-down agitation and guidance, this group may lead to organisational stagnation. Overall, this mode is great for execution but not ideal for complex problem solving and decision-making, which requires drive to go above and beyond.

Then there is the **"make magic happen"** mode — rare, and shown by perhaps 1 in 100 people consistently, where extreme ownership combines with initiative. They don't just take responsibility for what is; they take responsibility for what could be. They can see gaps and opportunities, mobilise others, and solve problems without waiting for permission or blessing from the boss. They're the ones you can trust with your critical 1% — because they'll own it end-to-end and find a way through, no matter how ambiguous or messy the situation. And then they'll find the next 1% and nail it too.

The difference between the top-right quadrant and the rest often comes down to ego and motivation. Ego distorts ownership. It makes people seek credit and shirk responsibility, or take responsibility selectively — only when it's safe. Good decision-makers keep ego in check by anchoring their sense of worth in progress, not praise. Being intrinsically motivated to achieve more is equally important. A team member who needs to be constantly re-inspired will require a lot more management effort to operate at their full potential compared to the one who is naturally excited about making things better.

Another distinguishing factor is that great decision-makers think in systems, not silos. They recognise how a single choice ripples across strategy, design, implementation and operations. They move comfortably up and down the decision-making pyramid — from high-level direction to operational detail — ensuring that the 1% they own connects cleanly with everyone else's.

The easiest way to spot your "make magic happen" people is to find those who run toward the "fire", not away from it, when things don't go to plan. When things go well, they shine the light on others. They take accountability without seeking credit, constructively challenge the status quo without recklessness, and push forward while keeping the whole system in view.

And the easiest way to grow more of them is to notice when someone starts moving in that direction — taking a bit more ownership, pushing a bit harder on a problem they didn't have to — and back them visibly.

The organisations that consistently bring out "make magic happen" behaviour in their people — by hiring for it, coaching for it, rewarding it, and removing the conditions that push people into the other three modes — will succeed.

Steve Jobs About Decision-Making at Apple (a transcript of a conversation with students at MIT in 1992):

"I've never believed in the theory that if we're on the same management team and a decision has to be made, and I decide in a way that you don't like, and I say "come on, buy into the decision, you know, buy into it. Look, we're all on the same team; you don't agree, but buy into it, let's go make it happen".

Because what happens is, you're paying somebody to do what they think is right, but then you're trying to get them to do what they think isn't right, and sooner or later, it outs, and you end up having that conflict.

So, I've always felt that the best way is to get everybody in a room and talk it through until you agree. Now that's not everybody in the company, but that's everybody that's really involved in that decision that needs to execute it.

That's how we try to run the company. The way we run it is we have a team at the top called the policy team. There are eight people on it. Mike is on it, I'm on it, and we have six other people on it.

We try to differentiate between the really important decisions and the ones that we don't have to make. The really important ones we work on until we all agree because we're paying people to tell us what to do.

I don't view that we pay people to do things; that's easy to find people to do things. What's harder is to find people to tell you what should be done. That's what we look for, so we pay people a lot of money, and we expect them to tell us what to do".

Make-Magic-Happen Teams

One person almost never cracks the 1% problems alone. The calls that truly move the needle are multi-dimensional, involving numerous domains from strategy, product and technology, to operations, legal, and finance. To land those big choices, organisations often need a small team or even multiple teams that can see the whole chessboard and act fast inside the broader enterprise.

There are lots of good books and frameworks about creating effective teams. Without trying to cram all the insights here, let's focus on just a few operating model aspects that are essential for teams to tackle the most critical problems.

First of all, great teams need to have end-to-end ownership of whatever problem they are working on, whether their scope is purely on working out a solution for the broader enterprise to implement, or covering the full cycle from strategy to delivery.

If the scope is manageable within a team, it's almost always better to assign the full strategy-to-delivery responsibility rather than have one team pass down a recommendation to another to implement. Wherever there are handovers between "upstream" and "downstream" teams, watch out for inherent conflicts when something doesn't quite go to plan — which happens in almost every project. However coherent your cross-team collaboration is, when things get dicey, you're bound to hear "their recommended solution makes no sense" and "they stuffed up the delivery". Often, these tensions are unproductive, creating friction. If it can be avoided through end-to-end ownership even at a cost of some functional duplication — benefits, in most cases, far outweigh the investment.

Setting the team up involves designing for two things at once: (1) the capability mix to solve the problem, and (2) the conditions that let the people in your team make the calls and execute without getting gridlocked or suffocated by the broader organisation.

Right Capability Mix

Let's start with the capability mix. In practice, there are two macro-skills you must have in the room:

- *Experts* (SMEs): people with deep domain knowledge and real-world scar tissue. They spot non-starters early. Albeit the leaders need to watch out for excess conservatism and "tried that — doesn't work" mentality. They understand constraints from regulatory to technological, can spot a risk from a mile away, and know which levers actually move outcomes. Good SMEs bring pragmatism and challenge constructively.

— *Problem-solvers* (strategists): people who can define the scope, frame the "exam question", break ambiguity into tractable choices, sequence analysis, and orchestrate a decision path. They keep the debate at the right level and ensure the team answers the right question, not the convenient one.

Great teams blend problem-solving horsepower + battle-hardened expertise. When one is missing, you get predictable failure modes. Raw horsepower without SMEs generates elegant answers that die on contact with reality. SMEs without a problem-solving toolkit optimise the current state and stall in incrementalism.

Horsepower Without SMEs Is a Road to Nowhere

A major bank once invested millions of dollars in a piece of brilliant consulting. A top-tier firm developed a sophisticated strategy and digital tool designed to reallocate business bankers' portfolios. The algorithm was elegant, crunching client data to align banker capabilities with client needs and growth potential. On paper, it looked like the bank had discovered a formula to unlock billions in new lending.

The executive team was excited. The strategy promised to optimise banker productivity, expand customer relationships, and deliver step-change growth. But when the solution was piloted in several regions, the results were underwhelming. Uptake was low, and frontline bankers resisted the changes.

The problem wasn't the mathematics — it was the culture. For decades, banker portfolios had been managed through an unwritten rule: when a banker left, the most senior and experienced colleagues inherited the best accounts, while juniors received less lucrative ones. Bonuses were tied to lending volumes, so the more established the clients, the higher the banker's pay.

Junior bankers understood that building their own books was part of career progression.

The new algorithm threatened to dismantle this system. Redistributing accounts based on "optimised growth potential" risked alienating top performers — many of whom could walk across the street to a competitor, taking valuable clients with them. This was a major risk that the bank wasn't prepared to take. What looked brilliant at the head office collapsed in the harsh light of frontline reality.

A handful of honest subject matter experts (SMEs) with lived experience could have flagged this issue early. With their input, the focus would have shifted from perfecting the technical portfolio reallocation to cultural and incentive transformation. Instead, millions were spent building a perfect algorithm that delivered little beyond perfectly articulated packs and well-formatted Excel spreadsheets.

Problem-solvers can develop beautiful narratives and dazzling models, but without pragmatic SMEs who ground solutions in real-world dynamics, strategy is little more than theory.

Business expertise is absolutely essential in quality decision-making, but unless it's coupled with strong problem-solving capability, whether in-house or external, it is likely to lead to suboptimal outcomes. Long-tenured experts, along with invaluable expertise and experience, carry a lot of "that's how we do things over here" baggage. It may lead to not seeing the forest for the trees.

When SMEs Tinker Instead of Transform

A major financial services administrator was responsible for processing millions of pension fund contributions every year. The contributions team alone had around 200 staff, most of them manually handling paper-based submissions.

The team was diligent and proud of their work. Each year they delivered incremental efficiency gains of around 5% through tighter rostering, better work allocation, and process tweaks. From their perspective, they were running a finely tuned machine.

When a new Chief Operating Officer (COO) arrived, he brought in consultants to take a fresh look. The consultants noticed something puzzling. During the end-of-financial-year peak, contribution volumes spiked to five times the usual weekly level. Yet the team managed to process the load without additional staff or overtime. Miraculously, in those two weeks, the SLA had never been breached.

Something didn't add up. The team, overseeing operational performance, couldn't explain how productivity could suddenly jump 5x in peak season but only improve 5% a year in normal times. When the COO examined the numbers, the truth became obvious: off-peak volumes could be processed by as little as 20% of their full-time staff.

The COO faced some stark choices: keep staffing year-round for the two-week peak (accepting 80% spare capacity for 50 weeks of the year), reduce staffing and extend SLAs during June spike, or introduce a more flexible staffing model that could surge during peak.

The contributions team's pursuit of marginal gains missed the real upside — an 80% productivity opportunity hiding in plain sight. Their deep expertise had narrowed their field of view to tinkering within the status quo. It took external problem-solvers to step back, reframe the issue, and reveal the true decision point.

SMEs ensure reliability and pragmatism, but without problem-solving horsepower they risk optimising the trivial. Step gains in value often come from challenging the frame rather than tinkering with the process.

Both macro-skills can be learned and occasionally, you may come across people who are strong in both: as a SME and a strategist. Often, these team members would also be high on "ownership" scale and sometimes on "proactivity". Anyhow, they're not common, so retain them, keep them engaged, and give them problems that matter!

Square-root talent

Let's take a small detour and revisit the price law that we discussed in chapter 3. When applied to human resources, it suggests that 50% of value is created by the square root of the workforce. It means that in an organisation of 10,000 staff just ~100 of the team members deliver half of the value. Let's call them "square-root talent". Let's admit it — we've all come across a few of those unicorns.

It's important to call out that while there's significant overlap, this is not the same as the «make-magic-happen» archetype we've just discussed. What distinguishes square-root talent is their ability to deliver exceptional outcomes in their domain of expertise. I'm a firm believer in the growth mindset — people aren't born as square-root talent; they develop into it through curiosity, deliberate practice, and the right opportunities. Leaders who recognise this potential early and invest in growing it will be rewarded many times over.

Unfortunately, unlike «froth talent» who talk a good game, real square-root talent doesn't always «bubble up» to the top. These rare people are often spread sparsely across organisational layers, so be on the lookout for those golden nuggets. Organisations that leverage their square-root talent — both the proven and the emerging — can achieve extraordinary results by focusing them on the one-percenters.

The Hire They Couldn't Afford Not to Make

Before tap-and-go was commonplace in Australia, a fintech startup was building a platform to enable retailers and food outlets to accept mobile payments and reward loyal customers. The ambition was significant, but funding was razor-thin — the founder was bankrolling it out of his own income.

One of the co-founders was a developer, and while he was exceptional, the task was far too large for one person to handle. The main founder, who was also a technology expert, found himself increasingly drawn into deep architecture and solutioning discussions, stretching him thin across commercial, operational, and technical fronts. He needed someone who could take full ownership of the iPhone app without hand-holding.

Rather than hiring someone affordable, he brought in one of the most experienced and expensive iOS developers in town. The team was stunned — it was unclear how they could sustain his eye-watering daily rates, which were three times the industry average. The founder was unwavering: "We can't afford to have anyone but top-percentile talent".

The talent decision paid off. Three months later, they had an end-to-end commercial-grade solution: a secure payments and loyalty platform, multiple point-of-sale integrations, and a customer app that matched the best in the category. Major retailers and financial services companies would struggle to deliver a comparable platform in two years with ten times the budget. Within months of launch, the working product helped them raise millions of dollars from private investors to scale internationally.

With macro-skills sorted, the next step is to ensure that the team is resourced with the right functional skills — sufficient to define the problem, work through the options and decisions, and, where applicable, implement.

The major challenge that many organisations grapple with in setting up teams to tackle important problems is bringing all the necessary functional expertise, without overexpanding to the point where the team becomes unmanageable.

Amazon CEO Jeff Bezos popularised a two-pizza principle, which is a good starting point in team design. The principle states that the team should be small enough to be fed with just two pizzas, typically between five to eight people. While I would not advocate for pizza as an office food of choice, cracking problems end-to-end in small groups works really well in my experience. To be successful, these small cross-functional teams need to have all the skills and authority to solve specific challenges or develop, deliver, and operate their specific product or service. They essentially operate like micro-enterprises within the larger organisation.

Depending on the scale and complexity of the problem or product the team is working on, the size could expand to ten-to-twelve, or even fifteen at a maximum. For instance, solving a problem involving both digital and non-digital features may require half a dozen developers and testers before you even get into product, marketing, operations, data, analytics, finance, legal, change management, and so on.

Whatever the team size, if there's research, analytical or development work involved it's important that all core members have a clear primary alignment to that team. The non-core team members, who only need to be involved episodically to review / validate things (e.g. legal, finance, risk) do not have to be 100% dedicated and can support multiple delivery teams. When it comes to the core members, who are doing the "heavy lifting", asking them to operate across multiple teams can be problematic due to conflicting priority management, context switching, and overlapping cadences. Transparency is also hard to maintain when a person sits on a number of teams creating room for shirking or hiding behind the busywork.

Unfortunately, we don't live in a world where budgets and resources are infinite, so having 100% dedicated team members may not always be feasible. However, when the resource sharing compromises are made, people need to have full clarity on which team and objective is their primary responsibility. The primary alignment does not need to be set in stone and can change, from quarter to quarter or sprint to sprint, but there should never be any ambiguity on what's going to give if contention arises.

Obviously, things can shift dynamically if an emergency arises in a secondary area. However, as long as the base settings are clear, it's a lot easier to manage exceptions if they arise, rather than manage and negotiate every team member's capacity on a daily basis.

Don't we all love a simple rule of thumb to cut through abstract concepts? Well, here's a practical one to try. If a team member is required to support a 1%-er more than 60% of the time they should be fully dedicated and offer spare capacity to other teams as available. If only 20-60% of their capacity is required, there needs to be clarity on their primary objectives and team alignment. Anything under 20% can be a shared resource coming to work as required.

Right Conditions

An equally important step in building effective teams is designing the right conditions for success. These teams should operate with a clear mandate, full ownership and authority over the problem, subject to guardrails.

Give them a simple and clear objective ("Reduce time-to-market by 60% for product X"), explicit constraints (regulatory red lines, budget, complaints tolerance), and ownership of the whole path from problem identification through to decision and execution. Within that frame, they should not need to ask permission for every step. However, they must make everything they decide and do radically transparent. More on the "How" in the next chapter.

If you find your teams constantly presenting their process, seeking guidance and approvals, you haven't built the right team or set the right conditions — you may have built an all-too-common corporate PowerPoint factory or what I call an executive entertainment unit.

In managing the teams, watch out for the HIPPO trap (Highest Paid Person's Opinion). Senior judgment is valuable when it clarifies goals, sets guardrails, or breaks through the deadlocks. However, it can be damaging when it pre-determines the answer or turns the decision-making and review forums into a performing art class.

In organisational behaviour, "authorship" is widely regarded as a more powerful driver than "ownership". If authorship is taken away by the HIPPO and all that is left is ownership of execution, it undermines empowerment, creativity and engagement. Like Steve Jobs commented in the example above — *The really important ones [decisions] we work on until we all agree because we're paying people to tell us what to do.*

Strong leadership, nonetheless, requires having full visibility of the decisions that the teams are making and the progress towards objective. In rare cases, senior interference can be justified, e.g. when the senior leader has information or expertise that can save the team a lot of analytical effort or help avoid a major risk. However, such "leadership override" should be an exception and the teams should be actively encouraged to push back if they experience excess contribution from their superiors.

Team Autonomy Without Transparency Is a Recipe for Disaster

It's not uncommon for organisations to go through the platform upgrade cycles. Unfortunately, those often don't go to plan.

A company was approaching end of support for its digital analytics platform. The technology stakeholders who reviewed the options realised that a strong digital analytics capability is also included in the enterprise content management system. It sounded like a perfect opportunity to "consolidate" analytics onto another platform and save few hundred thousand dollars in licensing fees.

For the tech team that was tasked with this initiative, it seemed like a perfect solution. The team planned and managed it as standard tech initiative without distracting other stakeholders. How hard can it be to set up a new platform and re-tag the website and mobile applications, right?

The reality turned out a lot more challenging than a recommendation statement on the PowerPoint slide. A seemingly simple and quick migration took almost a year to complete. The stakeholders across the business were caught unaware. It diverted a lot of capacity from other important projects, impacting multiple initiatives within the enterprise delivery pipeline. It crippled analytics capability with multiple teams "flying blind" for a period of transition.

And despite expectations, the cost savings were not realised, as it turned out that the legacy platform was still required to be maintained, as it was heavily used for marketing.

What went wrong? The decision was made by an autonomous team, but it was not transparent to the rest of

> *organisation. Had all the right stakeholders been involved at the start or at least had a full visibility of the recommendation, some of the assumptions that turned out to be false would have been challenged early and the decision or at least the approach would have been amended.*

If senior leaders want to change the team's course, they must change the destination or the guardrails or if nothing else helps — the people in the team — rather than undermining the work through micro-management.

Operating rhythm also matters. Unfortunately, there's no perfect one-size-fits-all cadence. Any operating rhythms that the team selects should focus on maintaining pace and creating transparency. In many cases, it will need to align in some way with the cadences of adjacent teams if there are any interdependencies.

There's usually a lot of attention dedicated to driving pace through cadences, however, the second important aspect — transparency — is often overlooked. Radical transparency approach that we unpack in the next chapter is arguably the most effective accountability enforcement mechanism. When all work, decisions and deliverables are visible, there's little scope for shirking. It also makes any weak links or bottlenecks within the team apparent.

A helpful tool to industrialise and embed transparency is cross-team showcases, where work-in-progress and choices or decisions get presented regularly, say at the end of each sprint. Showcases can be particularly powerful if they are an integral part of decision-making governance. As the work gets presented the team could be calling out specific choices they are considering or proposing to progress with. The forum has an opportunity to ask questions or challenge online or offline. Unless there are red flags identified during the showcase (or through post-showcase follow-ups) the team proceeds with its recommended course of action.

That's a super powerful "speak-now-or-forever-hold-your-peace" approach to decision-making governance. For many organisations it will require fundamental change in leadership mindset, organisational culture, governance and risk management. Worth noting that it's not suitable for every circumstance and decision. If the organisation is selecting a vendor for a $100 million dollar technology platform, flagging a recommendation at a cross-team showcase may not suffice. But for the wide range of "19%-ers" and even some of the less consequential "1%-ers" it can be a perfect ratification pathway.

Maintaining radical transparency takes effort. To minimise the "transparency" burden, the internal artefacts should be drafted to be brutally simple and readily sharable from the beginning. The litmus test is that internal decision-making paperwork should be understandable by the colleagues who only have general knowledge of the problem without having to provide a substantial amount of extra context. We'll discuss how to create transparency through clarity in more detail in the next chapter.

Finally, the dream team needs to be neatly stitched into the broader enterprise. Keep an eye out for the interdependencies that slow the decision-making progress. Often, the tension arises from working with the oversight and shared services functions such as architecture, legal, risk, internal audit, procurement, finance. The best antidote to friction is having clear delegates from those teams, who have full authority within their domain and share problem ownership and OKRs with the decision-making and delivery team.

Once the delegates are clear, they — just like the rest of the core team — need to have full forward visibility of the roadmap to a decision (or delivery), as well as the progress and choices made along the way. The No.1 rule for engaging with oversight and shared services teams should be "no skeletons or surprises".

Make-magic-happen teams should not be heroic. Heroism is nearly always a sign of a failure somewhere in the process or value chain. A well-functioning team working on 1% decisions should operate smoothly, leaning in collectively on tough matters and cruising through the easy bits.

Get the capability mix right, set the clear mandate and guardrails, keep HIPPOs in check, and run fast-paced and transparent cadences — and your team will be set up for success.

Culture is the force multiplier. The teams that are transparent, ego-light and insight-heavy are well-positioned to effectively tackle organisation's one-percenters. Next, we'll deep dive into the "How" of setting the right culture to unlock people's full potential.

Chapter 7:
The "How"

"Culture eats strategy for breakfast."

— PETER DRUCKER

The How: Culture of Focus, Openness, Clarity, and Speed (FOCS)

We've now covered the who of 1% decision-making. The next question is the one that most organisations under-estimate: How do you build an organisational culture that's supportive of effective decision-making?

That "how" is the difference between a team that produces a crisp, defensible decision in a matter of days — and a team that spends two months in discussions, and still ends up with a compromise answer nobody believes in or owns.

A talented team requires a high-performing organisational culture to enable quality decisions and effective execution of those. In its simplest form, organisational culture is a set of beliefs, values, and corresponding behaviours. The influence of culture on performance and decision-making quality is an important topic that would take a whole book to explore.

Here, we'll focus on the four most essential aspects of culture that, in my view, make or break effective decision-making and overall performance: Focus, Openness, Clarity, and Speed. You can think of those as four pillars that support decision-making (and to a large extent execution) effectiveness. This culture must be built on a solid foundation — capable, well-resourced and empowered teams, which we've discussed in the previous chapter.

Without that foundation, even the strongest cultural discipline won't compensate.

FIGURE 7.1: FOUR PILLARS OF DECISION-MAKING CULTURE

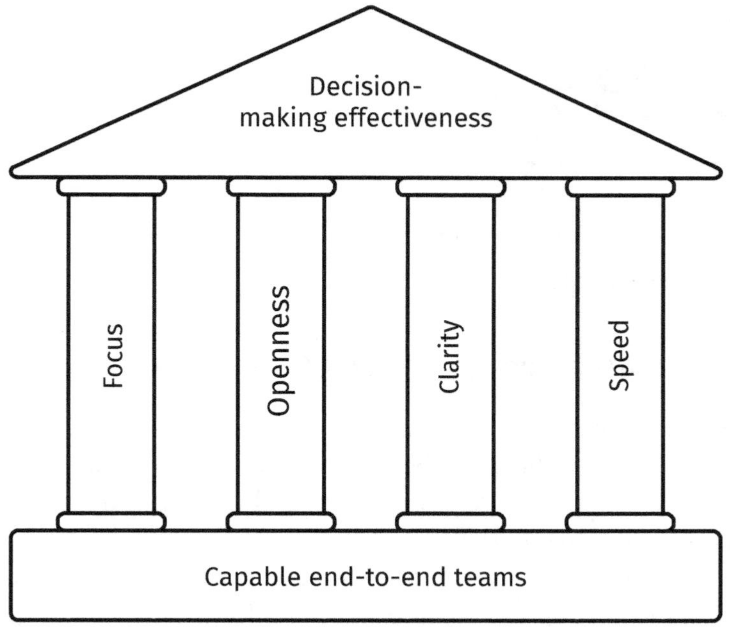

The four pillars set the conditions that stop teams from drifting into politics, noise, ego, rabbit holes, and optics management. When the organisation gets FOCS right, it doesn't just enable better decisions — it makes them faster, with less waste, and with firm commitment. It also sets a fertile ground for effective execution.

Let's break each pillar down into concrete actions and behaviours that you can start encouraging within your team or organisation.

Focus: Protect the Critical Path

Dispersion and distraction are among the biggest threats to effective 1% problem-solving. Your culture should be at work 24/7 making sure that the teams are spending their time on the right things. I've seen far too often how organisations, despite best intentions, experience a drift away from focus. Urgent but non-critical issues jump the queue. Instead of ruthlessly driving to an answer the teams spend days and weeks polishing the proverbial turd, risk aversion sparks endless circular debates, people start seeking comfort in solution-mode or unnecessary detail well before the exam questions are even framed.

Focus is the discipline of staying on the critical path and avoiding distractions. It means being ruthless about what matters first, and being comfortable to make some people, who want to take the conversation off the critical path, uncomfortable.

It all sounds well and good, so let's get into what steps and behaviours are required to bring this focus pillar to life.

Don't try to do everything and please everyone

By definition, focus requires concentration of efforts on the few most important issues. Most organisations that I've come across struggle with it. New great ideas and opportunities come up and get added to the slate. Risks and challenges emerge and remediation projects get squeezed in. The pipeline bloats, teams get overwhelmed with concurrent conflicting priorities, deadlines slip.

Unfortunately, there's no silver bullet for it. It comes down to being realistic about your capacity, having strict discipline about starting new work and ruthlessly pausing or stopping things that are no longer priorities.

Staying focused makes it impossible to please everyone. In reality though, this "pleasing everyone" is not a measure of success. It means taking on a lot, but not doing anything well. So, if we reframe it as "stuffing up many things" instead of "doing few things really well" it doesn't sound as confronting.

Something-for-Everyone Strategy

A large financial services organisation once developed an ambitious transformation program with a headline price tag of over half a billion dollars and strong expected returns over five years. On paper, it was an impressive strategy.

The program was carefully designed to be "inclusive" and offer something for everyone. Operations would receive a new workflow platform alongside a Lean Six Sigma toolkit. Distribution would get a modern CRM. Customers would benefit from new digital tools. IT would accelerate cloud migration and platform modernisation. Every major business unit could point to a line item that addressed some of its priorities.

As a result, no one objected. Senior stakeholders across the organisation supported the plan. There were no difficult trade-offs, no uncomfortable conversations, and no visible losers. From a political perspective, it was a success.

From an execution perspective, it was doomed.

The organisation didn't really have so much capital to invest. And even if it could raise enough capital, it didn't have the technical, managerial or organisational bandwidth to deliver that scale of concurrent change. Teams were already drowning in business-as-usual. Critical subject matter expertise was overstretched. Governance was slow and bureaucratic. The program tried to move too many pieces at once, without a clear critical path.

What was positioned to be a comprehensive strategy was, in fact, a collection of initiatives bundled together to avoid disappointment. It was an intellectual exercise rather than an executable plan. With no prioritisation or trade-offs, nothing truly mattered more than anything else — and when everything is a priority, nothing is.

Eventually, deadlines slipped, scope was revisited, and the ambitious program quietly unravelled into a portfolio of small business-led initiatives. The strategy didn't fail because it lacked vision — there was arguably too much of it. It failed because it lacked focus.

Strategies that try to please everyone rarely deliver for anyone. Focus requires trade-offs, and trade-offs require the courage to say no.

Catch the drift into tangential issues early

And when you do — pull back politely. Let's admit it, we've all been down the rabbit holes. There's almost never malice involved — often they are well-intentioned. A subject-matter expert is worried about an edge case. A leader has a pet idea. Someone wants to demonstrate competence and contribute to the conversation. Before you know it, a side comment turns into "let's just explore it for five minutes". Then five minutes become twenty. Then the meeting ends, without much progress on the critical issue.

A practical tactic: when a rabbit hole appears, name it, park it, and return to the what's on the critical path — in a respectful, constructive and non-personal way.

You can do it without offending anyone:
- "That's an important issue, but it doesn't feel like it's on the critical path for today's decision. May I suggest we park it and come back if the core answer depends on it?"
- "In the interests of time, to ensure we properly cover the key topic, I wonder if we could make a note of these concerns and ask X and Y to explore it offline and come back to this group if they believe it could change the answer?"
- "We're not saying, 'No.' We're saying, 'Now is not the best time for it.' Unless we find clear evidence that changes the answer. If so, we'll pull it back in."

These are not Machiavellian tactics, but genuine value protection. Leaders must ensure that their people's time and energy is used productively. If the team can't maintain focus, it will drown in distractions... and feel miserable for being busy while not achieving much.

Face the most painful issues first

If it itches — scratch. Most people and teams I know prefer to work on the easy non-controversial decisions. It feels productive and doesn't cause a lot of stress. But it also creates a trap: by picking the "low-hanging fruit" you're likely avoiding the issues that may deem those easy decisions irrelevant.

The uncomfortable truth is that the hardest and most contentious question or decision is often the most valuable one. It's the one that people deliberately or subconsciously avoid because it's messy, political, uncertain, or involves painful trade-offs.

Make it a norm that the team asks early:
— "What are the important issues we may be avoiding?"
— "Which issues / decisions do we think will be the hardest to resolve?"
— "What decisions or choices worry you most?"

Now, let me contradict myself for a minute. If you're facing into a series of tough decisions that need to be made, using a couple of less contentious ones as a warm-up is fine. It could help build a rhythm and make people feel good about the progress. But beware of turning a warm-up into procrastination. If the meeting ends and none of the painful decisions have been addressed, it's hardly a success. Reflect, call it out, and commit collectively to do better next time.

Sometimes focus means stopping work

Organisations tend to equate momentum with progress. But in 1%-ers, progress often requires courage to stop work that may feel productive, but isn't really moving the exam question (or decision) forward.

Here's the pattern you may recognise. A team starts working on a "quick win" to show momentum. The effort and time invested creates sunk cost. Sunk cost creates emotional attachment. Emotional attachment creates narratives that justify work in progress even if somewhere along the way it has become irrelevant to the bigger objective. With those collectively shared narratives, even asking "Should we stop?" becomes taboo.

High-performing teams do the opposite. They constantly evaluate the pipeline or work or decisions for how helpful it is in achieving the objective, and treat stopping work that's not well aligned as a sign of healthy progress.

A simple executive question that helps refocus by removing distractions is: "Given everything we now know and our objectives, what work could we stop, pause, or pivot?"

Openness: an Environment Where Truth Beats Ego

Focus keeps you on the right path. Openness determines whether you see what's actually on the path. Teams fail in decision-making when people hide concerns, soften truths, protect their turf, or defend their rusted-on positions. Not because they are mean — but because they are human. You can effectively counteract that in a way that preserves collaboration and pace through openness.

Trust is a prerequisite for openness. If trust is missing, people default to closed-shop safety mode, which is the opposite of what's required for effective decision-making. Invest in trust building and relationships within and across teams — it will pay off in spades.

The most explicit and powerful manifestation of cultural openness is what I call radical transparency.

Imagine a large, cross-functional team working on the all-important once-in-a-decade project to select a new technology platform. Team members from different departments such as IT, architecture, cybersecurity, procurement, legal, operate fairly independently connecting every second week with workstream updates. If cybersecurity identifies a show-stopper with one of the vendors, but doesn't share this insight until the next fortnightly forum it could result in two weeks of write-off work on the tech due diligence with that vendor. If product representative has concerns on the SLAs (service level agreement), but leaves those out of commercial discussion until the actual contract drafting, procurement team may not have negotiating levers to push for the tighter SLAs after the commercial terms have been agreed. If the legal team assumes that the contract will be with the global vendor, but procurement is dealing with the local authorised reseller, whose indemnities and guarantees are worthless, it could blow up into an unresolvable last-minute issue.

Radical transparency requires two-way commitment:

1) a person with information (or assumptions) that may be of value or concern for others must make it available to all relevant people (e.g. project team or even broader if required) as soon as practical.

2) a person who "has a say" including senior leaders, must come to the relevant forums or review incoming information and updates without delay.

Putting it into practice means ensuring that:

— Assumptions are written down in plain language and shared.

— Risks are called out early and acknowledged, without punishment or resentment.

— Options and decisions are logged, including why they were made.

— Dissenting opinions captured and understood, not suppressed or ignored.

In the example above, the cybersecurity team could have posted or emailed an update that one of the tech vendors failed their review as soon as it became apparent. Then it would be up to the procurement, tech and architecture representatives to ensure that no further effort is wasted on due diligence. If legal shared their assumption that all vendors must be able to contract direct to ensure strong indemnity protection, procurement team could have leaned earlier and either changed arrangements or removed some vendors from the short list.

Radical transparency often requires shifts in organisational culture, and can be challenging to some senior leaders. Instead of people coming to leaders for guidance and approvals, leaders come to the forums to stay across the work in progress and provide guidance where required. Instead of leaders holding on to information and drip-feeding it on a need-to-know basis to individuals, they share everything that could be helpful (subject to not breaking the law or compromising commercial outcomes).

The Spin Cloud

A former IBM intern once recalled his experience from the 1990's when he calculated twelve layers of management between himself and the CEO. Internally, the entourage of executives that shielded the CEO from anyone doing actual work was known as "the great cloud".

Each layer put a little spin on things to look good. One layer of spin is manageable. Twelve layers of compounding spin mean the CEO is making decisions in a fantasy world.

Contrast that with leaders who deliberately collapse layers, walk the floor and talk to the people closest to the problem. The information may be less polished, but it's real.

Extreme ownership that we discussed in the previous chapter, can work in the environment with constrained information sharing, but it is much more powerful in teams that operate with radical transparency. When work, decisions, assumptions, and trade-offs are visible, accountability becomes natural. People stop gaming the system because there's nothing to game — everything is out in the open. When everything is transparent, corporate politics gives way to collaboration.

There may be situations when certain sensitive information that could be of value to the team working on a decision can't be broadly disclosed. Treat those situations as exceptions rather than the base case — in my experience, "oversharing" produces far better decisions than "undersharing".

Assume positive intent — always

The fastest way to kill openness is to treat disagreement as hostility or stupidity. Once a room thinks it's unsafe to voice opinions or challenge, the meeting becomes a nodding performance. The suppressed disagreements and dissent eventually come out — either in the form of conflict or as a blow-up due to an oversight that hasn't been considered. The cost of fixing the disagreement later is significantly higher than facing into it early.

This is why establishing the principle of assuming positive intent across the organisation is so important. It can't be a hollow declaration, but needs be a deliberately reinforced operating mindset that is practiced daily. When someone pushes back, they're likely seeing a risk you've missed. If they disagree, they're working off a different assumption worth examining. If they're quiet, they may be holding the most valuable concern in the room.

A leader's job is to make that mindset visible, explicit and contagious. When you do, the room shifts from "debate as combat" to "debate as problem-solving". To facilitate it you may use introductions like this:
- Looks like there are two strong views on the matter. It's important that we explore and consider both to ensure that we collectively make the best decision.
- We haven't heard from everyone yet, now is a good time to present opposing views or concerns to ensure we don't miss anything important.

Leave the egos outside

The only winner should be your customer. Egos show up in subtle ways: the need to be right, the urge to take credit, the unwillingness to revise own view, the tendency to defend a team's work rather than examine it. When left unchecked, they could impact the pace or worse sway decision-making off the right course.

A practical reset that works surprisingly well is to explicitly anchor the room:

— "Let's make sure that the customer is the only winner of this conversation. Not any of us."
— "As a quick pulse check, if the customer is the only winner, which views or assumptions could we relax?"

It sounds simple, but it changes the psychology. A version of the first one can be used at the beginning of the meeting during context setting. The second could be used as a subtle reminder in the heat of the conversation. It gives people permission to let go of personal attachment to positions or ideas. Proactive "ego management" is an effective cure for turf protection that can be a major productivity killer, particularly in large organisations.

Unpack assumptions, not "mistakes" or "biases"

Many teams talk about "bias" as if it's a character flaw. Using that language explicitly or even in the internal dialogue, triggers "us vs them", "I'm right, they are wrong" mindset, which leads to defensiveness and shuts down learning. A more productive approach is to think and talk about differences in underlying assumptions or expectations.

Subtle language change can dramatically improve team dynamics and make decision-making more open and effective. Don't underestimate your own internal dialogue — by shifting how you personally interpret the opposing position, you shape your reactions and energy of the whole conversation.

Instead of: "Looks like you dislike vendor X?", try: "What assumptions are we making about the vendor X platform that makes it less attractive?" This small language shift makes it easier to be honest and invites curiosity rather than judgement.

Over years, I've come across many examples where conflicts erupt over unspoken and sometimes misunderstood assumptions. Below is an example where the delivery team was pushing back against investing effort in early testing of zero-points reward feature assuming it's a basic capability that their vendor wasn't concerned about... until UAT demonstrated it wasn't working. The failure was just an untested assumption that felt reasonable. In many cases, such assumptions are helpful, but when it comes to the one-percenters, they could be catastrophic.

The Assumption That Nobody Tested

A health company planned a flu vaccination campaign with a multi-channel marketing push and a new technology solution to distribute vaccination vouchers. Everything looked on track — until a critical "showstopper" surfaced.

The campaign hinged on creating a reward in the loyalty platform with a zero-points redemption rate, so customers could get vouchers without using their points. Given the importance of the campaign the project leader asked to ensure that the functionality is tested well in advance.

The team was not keen to invest effort in setting up a separate test. They assumed that zero-point reward will work the same way as other rewards, just with a "0" on the configuration screen. When asked, the platform vendor responded that they never tested it, but did not expect any issues.

Unfortunately, during the pre-release User Acceptance Testing (UAT), the reward didn't work. The platform simply could not handle a zero value in reward setup. What looked like a safe assumption turned into a major roadblock. The team had to rapidly develop a workaround, which delayed the campaign by a few weeks, missing the optimal campaign window.

A single unchecked dependency — left unvalidated because it "felt trivial" — turned an otherwise well-executed campaign into a headache. A couple of days to advance-test the feature could have saved several weeks of delay and many hours of rework.

Explore before explain: force the "I wonder…" reflex

Closely connected with all of the above approaches, openness requires a mindset shift from advocacy to curiosity. Jumping straight to advocacy brings resistance and creates tension that's premature and typically ill-informed. People start speaking to win the argument, not to learn and find the right answer. The antidote is to build a curiosity muscle.

Before explaining your view, explore the other person's logic until you're able to clearly articulate it:

— "I wonder what you're seeing that I'm missing."

— "Talk me through how you're thinking about it and the origin of your concerns."

— "What would need to be true for that to be the right answer?"

Sometimes the team argues about solutions because they don't actually agree on the problem. One of the powerful curiosity tools is the "Five Whys" technique that helps to dig through symptoms and get to the underlying driver.

The Five Whys of the Bird Droppings

For years, the U.S. National Park Service faced a persistent and costly maintenance problem at the Jefferson Memorial. The marble structure was deteriorating due to frequent cleaning with harsh chemicals, which was expensive and time-consuming. Excessive bird droppings were blamed for the costly maintenance. The obvious solutions were more frequent cleaning, bird deterrents, or chemical treatments — were all tried with limited success. The problem kept coming back.

Instead of treating the symptom, someone decided to dig deeper into "why".

That question led to a chain of inquiry using the Five Whys technique:

1) Why is the monument so difficult and costly to maintain?

— Because it constantly gets dirty due to huge number of bird droppings.

2) Why are there bird droppings on the monument?

— Because large numbers of birds congregate there.

3) Why do birds congregate at the monument?

— Because they feed on the insects that fly around the monument.

4) Why are insects attracted to the monument?

— Because powerful lights illuminate it at night.

5) Why are the lights on so early and so brightly?

> *— For aesthetic reasons, not operational necessity.*
>
> *The droppings turned out to be a symptom. The root cause of the problem wasn't birds — it was lighting. Delaying the lights by a couple of hours caused insect populations to drop, so birds moved elsewhere, and the droppings problem was largely resolved.*
>
> *No new cleaning contracts. No innovative chemicals. No bird-control systems. Just a better understanding of cause and effect.*
>
> *Leaders often skip this because it feels onerous and slow. In reality, it's a lot faster than solving the wrong problem.*

As the case study illustrates, when you make the best choice for the wrong problem well, you still fail. The genuine curiosity equipped with the right techniques (such as Five Whys) forces people to move past surface-level symptoms and uncover the true drivers of an issue. It's especially powerful in complex systems, where cause and effect are rarely obvious.

Initially, digging in and asking "why" repeatedly may feel superficial or rhetorical. But with practice it becomes natural. At the end of the day, it's all about ensuring you're solving the right problem before committing time, money, and effort to the solution.

Don't treat curiosity merely as a polite communication skill. It is a powerful decision accelerator. Genuine exploration reduces misalignment quickly because it reveals differences in mental models and assumptions, not just surface differences in opinions.

Clarity: Make Decisions Impossible to Misinterpret

Focus gets you to the right questions. Openness ensures that the truth comes out. Clarity reduces the friction of misunderstanding and maximises the chances of decisions surviving contact with the organisation.

A communication that is not clear is noise. A decision that is not clear is at best an intention and often a confusing one.

Simplify your message until a 10-year-old can follow the logic

Fine, make it an 18-year-old. Importantly this isn't about dumbing down or diluting the content. It's about boiling it down to what matters and removing ambiguity. If your message or decision requires jargon to sound credible, it's probably not clear.

You could employ a simple discipline: review the first draft and rewrite your communications until they are painfully simple. Then test the narrative with someone who isn't intimately close to the topic. If they can't explain it back to you, rewrite again.

When it comes to decision-making, simple and concise language is a force multiplier — it reduces cognitive load, guesswork and rework. It avoids politically correct ambiguity and reinterpretation.

Don't leave the room until everyone is on the same page

This is where many decision forums fail. People leave with different interpretation of the outcome, then proceed to execute different versions of the "same" decision. Weeks later, leadership wonders why delivery is messy. It's messy because the decision never converged.

Before closing, make all aspects of the decision explicit:
— what we decided to do
— what we decided not to do
— what we did not decide (i.e. yet to make a call)
— what assumptions our decision depends on
— what would cause us to revisit it (e.g. what new evidence could change the answer)
— what are the next steps and who owns those

This takes five minutes, but can save weeks or months.

Zero tolerance for high-level abstract agreement

Some leaders are masters of creating appearance of alignment despite the fundamental disagreements. What they usually do is lift the conversation to a high level of abstraction where everyone tends to agree. Imagine a debate where one stakeholder is against investing millions of dollars in a piece of technology arguing that there are lower cost ways to deliver the capability that their broad customer base needs. The other stakeholder has a strong preference for that particular solution as it allows their business unit to significantly accelerate speed to market for a particular customer segment. Instead of facing into this disagreement, a master-abstractor would say something like "It's great that we are all aligned on delivering the best personalised customer experience and ensuring speed to market. We obviously need to take into account the cost of implementation of the enterprise solution to deliver strong Return on Investment." While both stakeholders may feel heard, without facing into the disagreement the situation stays "hung up" or organically drifts in the direction where most energy is... which isn't always the right one.

If you hear "we broadly agree", "we're directionally aligned", "we've found common ground" — beware. It may feel comforting in the moment, but it will bite you down the track.

The job of a leader is not to create the illusion of an agreement. The real job is to expose the real disagreements and resolve them in order to come to the right decision.

A useful test question is: "If we had to make this decision tomorrow, what would we still be arguing about?" Whatever comes up is the real work.

Debate wholeheartedly, then commit — or define the path to commitment

Clarity doesn't require unanimous comfort, but it requires explicit commitment and clear next steps.

The worst meeting outcome is: "great conversation". No commitments. No actions. No owners. No deadlines. I've seen teams spend months analysing a decision, produce brilliant recommendations, then sit in 'great conversations' where nobody commits. By the time the opportunity window closes, the analysis becomes irrelevant.

The better pattern is:
1) Debate assumptions and options openly.
2) Present opposing and dissenting views.
3) Decide and confirm commitment ("Can everyone live with this?").
4) If not, agree on when and how to get to a commitment.

This is how adult decision-making works. It respects disagreement without being held hostage by it. We'll discuss this in more detail in chapter 9.

Speed: Move Before the Window Closes

Focus gets you to the right questions. Openness ensures the truth comes out. Clarity makes decisions stick. Speed — or pace, or expediency, whichever word you prefer — ensures all of that happens before the window of opportunity closes. Focus, openness, and clarity can all be done slowly and beautifully — and that's its own category of failure. A perfectly reasoned recommendation that arrives three months late is worth less than a well-reasoned one that arrives this week.

The 40-70 principle

In chapter 3, we introduced Colin Powell's rule of thumb: never decide with less than 40% of the information you need, but never wait for more than 70%. Jeff Bezos put the same idea more bluntly in his 2016 shareholder letter: if you wait for 90% of the information, you're probably being slow, and being slow is going to be expensive for sure.

His logic is straightforward. Many consequential decisions exist in a territory where you may have enough information to make a reasonable call but rarely enough to be certain. This remaining uncertainty can often only be resolved through action, not through another round of analysis. The 30% you don't know at the point of decision gets filled in by doing: launching, testing, observing, and adjusting. Deciding at 70% confidence and course-correcting as you learn is almost always superior to waiting for certainty that never arrives.

How much information is "enough" depends on the stakes. As a directional guide, the decisions in your "80%" bucket — the ones that matter least — should sit toward the bottom of the 40-70 range. Don't overthink them. Delegate, decide fast, move on. The "19%-ers" sit somewhere in the middle — enough rigour to avoid mistakes, but without boiling the ocean. For the genuine 1%-ers, you want to be closer to the top of the range — invest in getting the best available information, pressure-test your assumptions, but recognise that even for the most consequential calls, 70% in most cases is enough to act. Waiting for 90% confidence may mean the decision gets made for you — by competitors or by circumstances.

This is not a hard and fast rule, but it's a useful lens to keep the leaders and teams honest about where they are on the confidence spectrum and whether additional analysis is genuinely adding value or just deferring the discomfort of commitment.

High-velocity decision-making as a cultural norm

Maintaining high pace of decision-making starts with individuals, but needs to be an organisation-wide norm. Three practical levers make this real.

1) Match the process to the decision weight. We have touched on the common failure in large organisations, where they apply robust governance processes to inconsequential decisions. That's a bit like trying to race with a handbrake on. If the decision is reversible and the downside is modest, the process should take hours or days, not weeks. A good test is to ask yourself and the team "What's stopping us from making a call by the close of business today?"

2) Make indecision visible. In most organisations, indecision is invisible. It hides behind "still working through options" or "awaiting further input". Creating a norm where open decisions are tracked, aged, and reviewed forces the organisation to confront the accumulating cost of delay rather than letting it disappear into the backlog. As we discussed in the Clarity section of this chapter, every forum should end with either a decision or an explicit path to getting to one.

3) Set decision deadlines. Most organisations obsessively track when deliverables are due but rarely set explicit deadlines for when decisions must be made. The result is that decisions sit "in progress" or "under review" far too long, creating drag that nobody measures. Introducing "decision-by dates" into project cadences — particularly for the 1%-ers and 19%-ers — creates accountability for pace and makes the impact of indecision transparent.

Cost of waiting awareness

Every week a consequential decision sits unresolved, the cost compounds in ways that are hard to quantify and track on a dashboard. Teams can't plan, resources stay misallocated, optionality narrows as competitors jump at opportunities faster. And your "make magic happen" people disengage as they tend to have little patience for organisations and leaders that can't make up their mind.

Indecision is never free, but the cost isn't obvious. So, the trick is to put the "costs" of indecision — tangible and intangible — front-of-mind.

AI is making speed a different kind of challenge. Gathering the data, running analysis, and building options used to take weeks. Now you can compress these tasks to hours. That is incredibly powerful, but only if the organisation's decision-making process can keep up. The bottleneck in organisations is rarely about the speed of analysis. It is the speed of alignment, the willingness to commit with imperfect information, and the discipline to move decisively once the call is made. The organisations that will benefit most from AI-enabled speed are the ones that have the FOCS disciplines in place.

FOCS as an Operating System

Focus, openness, clarity, and speed sound simple because they are simple. But they are not easy. They require discipline — especially from leaders.

Most organisations drift toward the opposite: distraction, defensiveness, ambiguity, and sluggishness. That is why "1%" decisions are so often mishandled. If you want "make-magic-happen" outcomes, you need "make-magic-happen" behaviours in the room — and FOCS is the behavioural foundation.

Starting a First of its Kind Project

A major insurer decided to build a wellbeing program with elements of loyalty. Designing and building a loyalty program is a very complex task, but building it around wellbeing is twice as complex. Globally there were a few good exemplars of standalone wellbeing programs. There were also a lot of successful loyalty programs to take inspiration from. However, there was hardly any that effectively combined both. The team was facing a "first of its kind" complexity.

The first major challenge of projects like this is that the destination is undefined — the brief is so broad, you can design and build almost anything.

First few months of working out the design of the program felt like a drift. Lots of good conversations, lots of experts sharing experiences, lots of questions... lots of process without much progress. It wasn't uncommon for the team to come out of the meeting with more questions than answers. What should the program structure look like? What earn mechanics do we want? Which customers should be eligible? How much should the points be worth? Do points expire? The list went on...

Then there was a moment of realisation — the team needed to focus on the toughest questions first. Rather than debating a large number of issues every time they met, they compiled a list of about half a dozen of the most hotly debated ones and captured views of different stakeholders on what they thought the right answer was. Having a documented short list of the most "painful" questions was cathartic.

The team then organised a fortnightly meeting with a very creative title: "decision-making forum", which included senior stakeholders with a say across the business (key General Managers and Heads of). The key to those forums was to foster an open and robust conversation about the (1) questions, (2) options, (3) recommendations and (4) considerations / risks.

The conversations were often heated. Some stakeholders were pushing for more conservative settings (e.g. restricting access to select products only), while others were keen to drive growth (e.g. by opening up to all products to maximise target audience). Some were more comfortable with risk (e.g. offering more generous points expiry rules), others pushed for tighter commercial settings to reduce potential exposure.

The key was to keep reminding people about the need to assume positive intent and to invest time in understanding each other's viewpoints and underlying assumptions. Often, after the assumptions were uncovered and discussed, emotional intensity subsided, and alignment emerged.

> *The team made sure the decisions on the recommendations were clearly articulated and documented to avoid any misinterpretation. The team also pushed hard to maintain fast pace — if a discussion was stalling — they moved to the next item and addressed the hiccup offline.*
>
> *The team were explicit about not locking the "decision" until all ambiguity got cleared — it often took one conversation with the dissenting voice and clarification at the following meeting. This way everyone was comfortable they were heard, the risks were considered and a collectively owned decision was made.*
>
> *Was everyone happy with every decision? Hell no. Some thought the earn settings were too generous, others worried about expiry rules, a third group worried about explaining nuanced eligibility. But as a package, everyone agreed the program design was the best it could be despite its imperfections.*

We'll come back to this hypothetical insurer-led wellbeing rewards program a few times in the chapters ahead — it's a useful running example because it touches almost every tool in the method.

There is a Zen Buddhist saying: "How you do anything is how you do everything". It applies to decision-making. The disciplines in this chapter (focus, openness, clarity, and speed) are not tools you pick up for the big occasions and put down for the rest. They are daily habits, and good habits should not have an on-off switch. How you handle the hundred small decisions trains the reflexes you'll rely on for the ones where it counts most. This obviously doesn't mean every decision deserves the same process and rigour, but the behaviours — the willingness to name the real question, to invite dissent, to commit clearly and move at pace — those need to be consistent regardless of the dollar figures at stake. Scale the process to the decision. Never scale down the discipline.

That consistency is also the best protection against the failure patterns we'll examine in chapter 11, where we'll map the organisational and psychological forces that erode decision quality, which often happens so gradually that no one notices until the damage is done. For now, it's enough to recognise that FOCS isn't just a framework, it's a way of operating. And the surest way to make it stick is to practice it everywhere, not just where it feels consequential.

How you make one decision is how you make every decision. Make it count.

Having covered the "who" and the "how" of decision-making, we can progress to the "why" and the "what". In the next two chapters, we'll explore a practical approach to making the critical decisions. We'll also continue exploring potential failure points: unclear objectives, wrong questions, fake options, analysis paralysis, decision overload.

Chapter 8:
The "Why"

"If you don't know where you are going, any road will get you there."

— LEWIS CARROLL

If I'm being honest, a more fitting title for this chapter would have been "The Frame". Because that's what it's really about — framing the decision before you attempt to crack it. But I didn't want to let an odd noun spoil an otherwise perfect line-up of "Who", "How", and "What" headlines. So the "Why" it is. It's not a bad fit either, because everything in this chapter is about answering the question that too many teams skip: why are we solving this particular problem, in this particular way, with these particular measures of success?

This chapter covers the essential groundwork that must be laid before any analysis begins. We'll start with objectives and key results (OKRs). To be clear, we are not talking about the watered-down corporate variety, but the kind that actually forces clarity on what success looks like and how you'll know you've achieved it. Then we'll move to constraints. These are the non-negotiable boundaries that define the edges of your decision space. We also talk about the guiding principles that, unlike the corporate poetry you'll find on most strategy decks, are sharp enough to shape the outcome. Finally, we'll tackle what is arguably the hardest and most impactful step in our decision-making method: formulating and prioritising the right questions. Because if you're solving the wrong exam question, even the most brilliant analysis won't save you from failing.

We'll open with a case study that brings all of this to life and illustrates what happens when a team skips the "why" and goes straight to the execution.

A Bumpy Road to Customer Trust

A major telecommunications company experienced a series of incidents and events that led to deterioration of customer trust. It also had an impact on advocacy, making it harder to retain and acquire customers.

What do big companies do when there's an issue? They create a business unit to solve it. Got productivity concerns? Set up a productivity task force. Lagging in AI? Launch an AI function. Customer churn is on the rise? Build a retention squad.

The new business unit was tasked with a lofty goal of rebuilding customer trust by coordinating cross-business efforts and driving relevant technology uplift. And rebuilding they did. Working closely with architecture the team identified an opportunity to implement a world-class consent management platform that would allow near-infinite flexibility to collect and manage customer consents — be it for sensitive data handling or marketing activities.

Not only would this new platform be able to solve the current and future business needs, it would also make it easier to stay compliant with any future regulations in the privacy space.

The team commenced a formal selection process, screened a number of vendors and selected the one that offered maximum flexibility and future proofing.

The project was full steam ahead in the final stages of negotiation with the vendor — ready to sign the contract. As the contract signing decision was fast approaching a number of difficult questions came up from other business units:
— What problem are we actually trying to solve with the platform?

> — *What benefits will justify the multi-year build and multi-million investment?*
> — *What's the impact on the enterprise delivery pipeline of integrating half a dozen platforms tightly enough for this technology to work?*
> — *What alternatives (to a new platform rollout) have been considered?*
>
> *Facing those uncomfortable questions so late in the project was akin to trying to stop a 200-wagon iron ore train. Noble ambition, huge momentum, project team mobilised, world leading technology vendor ready to sign the contract. All great, except missing clarity on "why" and "why in this particular way".*
>
> *With an impending multi-million-dollar and multi-year decision, the company was facing one of the toughest dilemmas in its history.*

This chapter will unpack a holistic decision-making approach that puts the horse before the cart and helps avoid challenging situations like the one above. We'll come back to this case study to illustrate a better way to approach the most consequential decisions more effectively.

The approach that we'll go through does not intend to be one-size-fits-all or a rigid set-in-stone process. A better way is to consider it a toolkit that can help frame really complex enterprise choices. Smaller team-level or individual-level decisions, even if they are 1%-ers, may not require the full toolkit — just a couple of steps should be sufficient.

Setting the Path: OKRs, Constraints and Guiding Principles

One of the most common reasons decision-making fails comes down to a lack of clarity about what success actually looks like and how progress will be measured. To make effective calls along the way we need to be clear where we're heading. Many leaders assume their teams either "get it" when they outline a high-level vision or "will sort it out" through the process. But without clear, precise, measurable anchors, objectives can lead to a lot of well-meaning activity without real progress.

So, the first essential step in high-stakes decision-making is getting all relevant stakeholders, from senior leaders to those who actually do the work, crystal clear on the objectives, key results, constraints and guiding principles.

Start with the Objectives... and Key Results

The theme of this book is making disciplined, conscious decisions — especially in complex, high-stakes environments. This is where the Objectives and Key Results (OKR) framework shines.

There are multiple frameworks focused on objective setting and performance tracking such as balanced scorecard, KPIs (Key Performance Indicators), KRAs (Key Result Areas), to name a few. I find that the OKRs methodology is by far the most effective tool when it comes to decision-making. It forces leaders to define the destination in a way that is both aspirational and measurable. The objective part answers: Where do we want to go? The key results part answers: How will we know we're getting there?

Most importantly, OKRs create a built-in decision filter:
— If a choice moves you closer to the objective and improves at least one key result, it's probably worth pursuing.
— If it doesn't help, or worse, if it undermines another key result, it's a signal to rethink where that choice fits and whether it's worth stopping or pivoting.

Well-defined and well-managed OKRs help maintain focus, prevent drift, resist reactive decision-making, and keep the organisation aligned on purpose — not just "going through the motions".

OKRs vs KPIs

A lot of leaders confuse OKRs with KPIs or treat them as interchangeable. They're not.

KPIs (Key Performance Indicators) are performance measures that track the health of ongoing operations. They're like the vital signs of the business: revenue, churn, NPS,

The process of defining OKRs starts with the objective (the "O" part). The objective is the headline — the statement that frames the desired outcome or ambition. Depending on the importance of decisions that you are planning to use these OKRs for, the objective could be broad and bold or narrow and conservative. However, the main requirement is that it needs to be specific enough that people know when it has been achieved.

Good objectives have three qualities:

1) Aspirational — ambitious enough to push beyond business-as-usual.
2) Clear — unambiguous, so everyone interprets it the same way.
3) Time-bound — it should be possible to achieve within a defined period (e.g. a quarter, year, or program phase).

An objective should not read like a KPI. It's not "reduce costs by 10%" or "implement new CRM". Those are tasks or targets. A strong objective reframes the intent at a higher level — so the measures serve it, not define it.

Imagine a company embarking on a major transformation program aimed at achieving sustainable cost savings without harming its competitive edge. This is the kind of situation where a vague goal ("cut costs by 10%") could lead to short-term wins but long-term damage.

A well-structured objective might look like this:

Deliver $50 million in sustainable cost savings by the end of financial year while preserving — and strengthening — our core differentiating capabilities.

In the case study that we introduced at the beginning of the chapter the implied (not formally defined) objectives would have been something like:

— At the business unit level: turn around customer trust by coordinating cross-business efforts and driving relevant technology uplift.

— At the initiative level: implement world-class technology to manage privacy and consents providing flexibility and future proofing the business.

As you can see, both tick the aspirational box, but are hardly clear or time-bound. The better versions of the objective would have been:

— At the business unit level: bring customer trust to the level of key competitors within two years, by coordinating and supporting cross-business efforts.

    NB: technology is one of the potential solutions, but it does not need to be hard-wired into the objective, as there is a risk that this might bias the decision-making.

— At the initiative level: cost-effectively strengthen privacy and consent management within a year, ensuring it's in line with risk appetite. NB: again, world-class technology is one of the pathways to achieving objective, but the real objective is ensuring the business operates compliantly and within its risk appetite.

Once the objective is set, the next step is to define three to five key results (the "KRs" part) — measurable outcomes that, taken together, would demonstrate the objective has been achieved. Some treat KRs as a to-do list, which isn't the right approach. They are the evidence that the aspiration has been realised.

The key results should be:

— Outcome-focused — not activity-focused.

— Specific and measurable — so that it's possible to objectively assess whether they are achieved or not.

— Stretching the team without being impossible — the last thing you want is to drive disengagement and resentment by setting wildly unrealistic expectations.

— Clear of "vanity metrics" that look good on paper but say nothing about real progress.

Continuing with the transformation program example above, the key results could be something like:

1) Achieve $50 million in verified, in-year cost reductions, independently validated by Finance.

2) Maintain or improve customer net promoter score (NPS) in our top three service lines.

3) Retain at least 95% of top-performing talent in critical capability areas.

In this case, the KR part of the framework achieves three things. It makes the ambition explicit and time-bound. It balances financial outcomes with customer and capability outcomes. And finally, it protects against destructive cost-cutting that erodes what makes the business competitive.

Measuring the Wrong Thing

Contrast that with what happened at a large financial services administrator during its troubled core platform transformation program. One of their key measures of progress for the program was "lines of code written".

On the surface, this metric felt tangible. Millions of lines of code were being delivered by the offshore tech vendor. But in reality, those lines of code weren't functional, didn't integrate into a working platform, and failed to deliver the outcomes the system was designed for — even after five years of development.

"Lines of code" was a classic activity metric — it measured effort, not impact. It told the team they were busy, but it said nothing about whether they were actually building the right thing or moving closer to the program's intended outcomes. Worse, it created a perverse incentive to write more code, not better code.

The result: a lot of progress on paper, but very little progress in reality.

Going back to our consent platform initiative example, the decision-making around the path to achieving the objective would have been easier with a few clear key results. Potentially something of this nature:

1) Privacy and consent management are compliant and within risk appetite based on the Legal team assessment.
2) The cost of maintaining compliance is within the current budget plus or minus 10%.
3) The customer-facing elements of the solution are fully transparent, simple to understand and minimise friction — to be validated through customer testing.

The final critical step in OKR development is to prioritise. Unfortunately, this step often gets missed. It's all well and good to have aligned objectives and clear key results that underpin those objectives, but when it comes to complex decision-making not all Os and KRs are created equal. Sometimes, the conflicting trade-offs will bring it down to which objective or key result comes first, and which one we are a bit more comfortable missing.

In our example above, there are three Key Results for consent platform initiative. However, when ordered consciously, the priorities may shift. Having compliance and risk appetite alignment is a non-negotiable, so the No.1 spot is perfectly justified. However, when it comes to budget (No.2), the company may have more flexibility. For example, they could aim for +/-10%, but would tolerate a 15-20% budget overrun if it could be traded off against opportunities to improve transparency and simpler user experience (No.3).

Constraints: the Boundaries Not to be Crossed

If objectives define what "good" looks like, constraints define what is non-negotiable. Constraints are often regulatory, financial, ethical, operational, or time-bound limits within which the decision must sit. For the major enterprise decisions, they are not optional — they shape the feasible solution set.

For smaller or compliance-focused choices, constraints can be built into the OKRs, like we saw in the section above.

One of the most common and costly mistakes in decision-making is confusing constraints with objectives. When this happens, organisations optimise for the wrong thing, usually because a risk-averse team has quietly redefined the problem.

For example, if a conservative legal team leans in to define the objectives of a project, they may articulate not an objective but a constraint: "Minimise legal risk exposure", "Avoid regulatory risk", "Ensure best in class privacy compliance". These are better suited to be guardrails, but not the goals. If compliance is treated as an objective rather than a constraint, the business will be maximising compliance, while trying to minimise adverse impact on commercial outcomes. If we do the right thing and treat compliance as a constraint, we focus on the business objective of growing revenue, launching a product or reducing cost, while ensuring we are compliant.

Mislabelled constraints lead to zero-risk thinking — an approach that almost always results in zero progress. Good decision-makers make constraints visible, name them explicitly, and prevent them from hijacking the objectives. A constraint is not a direction; it is a boundary. It answers the question: "What must be true for an option to be considered acceptable?"

Guiding Principles That Actually Guide

Most companies love the idea of "guiding principles". Strategy consultants spend weeks on high-profile projects defining and refining those. The problem? Most of them aren't really guiding anything.

I'm sure you've seen those principles on the glossy posters in the strategy decks and on the About pages of corporate websites. They sound inspiring, but they're often so broad and agreeable that they could apply to any organisation, any project, any time in history. They make for nice wall art but are useless when you're staring down a hard enterprise decision.

Here's a sample of the kind of "guiding principles" I've seen on dozens of projects:

1) We must put customers first.
2) We will always act with integrity.
3) We always deliver value.
4) We future-proof the solution.
5) We work together as one team.

These are fine values. Nobody's going to stand up in a meeting and argue: "Actually, I think we should put customers last and act without integrity".

And that's exactly the problem. If there's no debate, there's no edge. If everyone nods along, it's not a decision-making tool, but a piece of corporate poetry. Real guardrails aren't meant to make everyone feel good. They're meant to help everyone choose. And choosing means trade-offs, disagreements, and discomfort.

The most frustrating part is that organisations spend a lot of time and effort polishing these principles. And often the result of such polish is the opposite of what's required. The team starts with something crisp and specific like "the solution must be radically simple from a customer UX perspective" and then through iteration and input from senior stakeholders they drift towards abstract and toothless: "We will design a solution with the customer at the centre".

Why Guiding Principles Matter

Similar to constraints that we discussed above, guiding principles must help clarify the path to the objective. Their role is to actually guide decision-making in uncertain high-stakes environments, where there can be multiple right answers. One way to look at it is to treat them as initiative-level values that you operationalise through decision-making.

They're most powerful in situations where:
— There's no clear quantitative answer.
— Multiple competing options have merit.
— You're making a call with a high level of uncertainty or ambiguity.

Good guardrails let you ask: Which option stays true to (or best aligns with) our guiding principles? Which one violates them (or is least aligned)? When the maths is inconclusive, the guiding principles light the way.

Guiding Principles That Make a Point

Let's take a hypothetical insurer that wants to design a wellbeing platform with its own rewards currency. Programs like this are complex, involving product design, technology, partnerships, compliance, and marketing all moving in parallel. Most decisions don't have a spreadsheet answer.

If the project team takes guiding principles seriously, they can become an essential pathfinding tool — not a «tick the box» exercise.

To get to the right set, the team may intensely debate options and wording. It's not always quick, and it's certainly rarely painless. But it's worth it. At the end of the process, the team may have crystallised half a dozen non-negotiables and ordered them by importance. Among those could be things like:

— As simple as possible

— Radically transparent

— In service of customer health

Notice something? While you can agree with all of them in principle, when you get into real design decisions, these can (and will) create constructive tension. That's the point.

Picture this: shortly after landing these principles, the team gets approached by a fuel retailer with a compelling discount offer that would be appealing to many customers. The pitch is slick and the numbers are attractive. However, it would only take the team a minute to make the call. The offer doesn't align with one of the guardrails — it isn't in service of customer health. No matter how tempting it is, it's an automatic no-go.

Another likely debate during program design could be the redemption value of a point. Some might argue for the pricing approach used by supermarkets and credit card loyalty schemes — typically around 0.5 cents per point. Others might push for a variable redemption value depending on the reward, similar to airline frequent flyer programs. A third group might advocate for the flat 1 cent per point model that most traditional retail loyalty schemes rely on.

There would be no obvious «right» answer. Financial models might lean towards the lower-cost or variable options. But once the team puts the choice through the guiding principles, things become clearer:

— A variable value per point would make the program complex to understand and explain — failing the principle of simplicity.

— A 0.5 cent model could inflate perceived value but under-deliver on actual worth — failing the principle of radical transparency.

— A flat 1 cent per point is clear, simple to communicate, and honest — passing both principles.

The decision makes itself — once the team puts it through the guiding principles.

If your guiding principles don't create disagreement during development, they're not helpful. And here's the test: When you present them to a group of smart, informed stakeholders, do they start arguing about which one takes priority in a given scenario? Do they challenge the wording? Do they worry about unintended consequences?

If yes — you're on to something. You've found the friction that forces clarity. If no, you've just churned out another set of motherhood statements. Add them to the corporate intranet where they can gather dust.

Building a Set of Guiding Principles That Work

1) *Start with the hard decisions you know you'll face. If you're building a product, you might face trade-offs between speed, quality, and cost. If you're launching a service, you might wrestle with scale vs personalisation.*

2) *Phrase them so they create tension. "We put customers first" isn't tension.*

3) *"We prioritise customer simplicity over operational efficiency" is tension — because someone is going to disagree.*

4) *Order them by priority. Lack of prioritisation or weighting is counterproductive. In the wellbeing rewards program example, simplicity came first for a reason. The underlying insurance product is incredibly difficult to understand with a variety of covers and complex inclusion and exclusion criteria. So, the team felt that the customers wouldn't forgive the company for adding more complexity to their products. That is why simplicity trumped all other principles when conflicts arose.*

5) *Pressure-test them. Take a live decision and run it through the guiding principles. If it doesn't change or clarify the outcome, the guardrail is either irrelevant or too vague.*

6) *Use them in the wild. Guiding principles are useless if they're not part of the everyday language of decision-making. If you're not hearing them referred to in debates, they're probably ornamental, not operational.*

Guiding principles in action

Without real guardrails, ambiguous decisions where there's no clear "analytically correct answer" are made in several suboptimal ways. By default — whoever speaks last, loudest, or has the highest title wins. By precedent — "We've always done it this way" becomes the deciding factor. Or by inertia — nobody wants to make the call, so nothing changes. In all those cases, the business surrenders to drift instead of making a decision.

The magic of well-crafted guiding principles is that they create alignment without needing a senior leader in the room overseeing and course-correcting every discussion. They empower teams to make values-consistent decisions without escalating every question upward.

Imagine two teams faced with the same ambiguous problem. One has guardrails, one doesn't. The first makes a decision in a day, confident it fits the agreed principles. The second holds three meetings, escalates to leadership, and still delivers a watered-down compromise. The presence (or absence) of a decision-making scaffold can make a huge difference.

Guiding principles are meant to be enduring over the life of the project, but they don't have to be set once and for all. The environment changes, business models evolve. What was once a clear constraint might become irrelevant or even counterproductive.

If you're finding that a guiding principle...
— is never referenced in decisions,
— never rules out an option,
— or is something that everyone always agrees upon instantly...
...it may be time to review and refresh. Maybe it has become too safe. Maybe it has outlived the decisions it was meant to guide. In either case, consider replacing it with something sharper.

When it comes to deciding on the 1%-ers, good guiding principles keep the project in the right lane, moving at speed, when the fog rolls in and the map runs out. If they're not making you and your team pause, debate, and sometimes squirm, they're not doing their job.

If OKRs, constraints and guiding principles are the necessary first step in high-stakes decision-making, formulating the questions (or actual decisions to be made) and prioritising their importance is arguably the hardest and probably the most impactful in terms of getting to the right answer. We'll use questions and decisions interchangeably.

Asking the Right Questions

Let's start with the questions. In the design and delivery of complex enterprise initiatives there can be dozens or even hundreds of major choices or decisions involved. Those choices are often interconnected with a complex web of dependencies. It can be daunting for the team to tackle such complexity without clarity on where to start.

As we discussed in the focus section of the previous chapter, the best way to start is almost always with the most difficult and debatable set of questions.

Keep track of the discussions and compile a list of the issues that either get most hotly debated, or worse, actively avoided due to contention.

In the case of the wellbeing rewards program, those would be questions like:
— What is the high-level program structure?
— Should it be built in-house or licensed from an established operator?
— What should be the value per point?
— Which customers should be eligible to participate?
— How much value should we invest in rewards based on the expected returns?
— What earn mechanics should be employed to maximise cost management flexibility?

In our transformation program example, the questions could be:
— Which capabilities are critical to growth and must be excluded from cost out?
— Which parts of business would benefit from technology investments most?

- Which implied constraints can we relax to unlock the value (e.g. spin-off an underperforming business, dramatically simplify product set)?

In our consent platform example, we could ask the following:

- Which features/capabilities are required to strengthen privacy position and reduce consent management risk?
- What is the cost-effective way to deliver those features or capabilities?
- How much are we prepared to invest in future-proofing before the upcoming regulatory changes are defined?

An important point of caution in formulating the questions is to avoid anchoring those to a solution prematurely. Take our consent platform example. The project team started their work with a set of questions, which presupposed the need for a new technology platform is a given, e.g. "which is the most flexible and future proof privacy and consent platform to implement". Had they started with a different question — such as "what's the most cost-effective way to strengthen privacy and reduce consent management risk?" — they would have ended up on a completely different path.

When it comes to defining questions, stick to the principle of "falling in love with the problem, not the solution". A good tool to keep in mind is a popular business communication framework: SCQA (Situation, Complication, Question, Answer). Spend time understanding the situation and the complication parts before landing on the actual question that you need to answer. Otherwise, you risk stepping into the wrong track from the start.

Once the questions are known, it's often helpful to order those based on importance. The most important ones, the "exam questions", are often those that have the most interdependencies, so it's best to try and tackle those early to unlock decision-making across the broader set.

In our wellbeing rewards program example, unless the team could confirm that the program would be currency-based with points redeemable for rewards (as opposed to say status-based or tenure-tiered), we couldn't progress to the next layer of questions such as value per point, expiry rules and earn mechanics. The question set and options for a status-based program would look quite different.

It's worth noting that the questions may differ in terms of the type of answer they require. Some will lend themselves to a choice of one of multiple options (e.g. point pricing approach as we saw earlier in the chapter), others may be binary (e.g. go vs no-go decision on the investment opportunity), others could be qualitative descriptions (e.g. list of departments impacted by cost-out initiative) or quantitative figures (e.g. investment project budget). Those questions can be tackled using the techniques discussed in the next chapter.

Ensuring Exam Questions Are Covered

But before we get to cracking the problem, we need to ensure that all "exam questions" are covered. The three essential litmus tests, that you may recall from our Chapter 4 on how to identify the critical 1%, are:
— What are the most critical assumptions we are relying on?
— What are the potential show-stoppers?
— What are the potential game-changers?

FIGURE 8.1: THREE LITMUS TESTS

Litmus test	What are the potential show-stoppers?	What are the most critical assumptions?	What are the potential game-changers?
To ensure that the outcome…	… doesn't fall significantly short of expectations	… has good chances of meeting expectations	… has potential to significantly exceed original expectations

These three tests map to the three potential outcome bands. Validating the most critical assumptions gives confidence in achieving the expected outcome. Surfacing potential show-stoppers flags the risk of falling short. And spotting potential game-changers reveals scope to deliver above expectations.

The Cheapest Way to Validate the Most Critical Assumptions

A Private Equity business was exploring opportunities in online ordering and home delivery of prescription medications. The space looked hot: several start-ups were pitching partnership and M&A opportunities. Newspaper headlines were buzzing with stories of imminent digital disruption of pharmacy sector. On the surface, the two choices seemed clear — either buy one of the start-ups or partner by integrating ordering and delivery services into one of the portfolio businesses in healthcare.

Instead of rushing to kick-off an M&A due diligence or partnership negotiation, the leadership team paused and did something much simpler: they spoke with a handful of industry experts. In those conversations, the real issue quickly surfaced. As it turned out, despite fancy tech, all those start-ups really struggled to scale.

The challenge they faced was that the most valuable consumers of prescription medications were senior 70+ year-old customers. For them, a regular trip to the pharmacy wasn't a hassle — it was part of their weekly or monthly routine and a valued opportunity to socialise. Most of them knew their pharmacist personally. Meanwhile, younger and more "digital-native" customers placed orders only occasionally, usually for small and low-margin baskets like antibiotics or contraception pills. The frequency and basket size were so low that no sustainable business model could be built from them at scale.

What looked like an exciting growth market on paper turned out to be a structural dead end. By validating the most critical assumptions through a few targeted conversations, the business saved itself millions of dollars in wasted investment and months of effort building an MVP through a portfolio company that was destined to fail.

Sometimes, the cheapest, most effective way to validate assumptions is a coffee catch-up with the right people.

Now that we have a set of important questions or decisions to make, we can proceed to working out the answers.

Chapter 9:
The "What"

"The formulation of a problem is often more essential than its solution."

— ALBERT EINSTEIN

If the previous chapter was about framing the problem, this one is about cracking it. Finally! — you may be thinking. If you've been itching to skip past the objectives, constraints, guiding principles and exam questions and get straight to the answer — I get it. But as the consent platform case study in the previous chapter showed, jumping to "what" without nailing "why" is how organisations come close to signing multi-million-dollar contracts for problems they haven't properly defined.

Now that you've done the hard yards, you have clear objectives, prioritised key results, well-defined constraints, sharp guiding principles, and a set of exam questions that need answering. The stage is set. This chapter walks through the analytical process of getting to the answer: from generating real options (not the dressed-up dummies that make the predetermined choice look sensible) through to structured analysis, recommendations, debate, commitment, and execution.

If you aren't yet sick of my metaphors, think of it this way: the "Why" makes sure you're pointing the telescope at the right part of the sky. The 'What' is the discipline of working out exactly what you're looking at — and what to do about it. Both are applied fresh each time a new consequential decision comes up, but without the first, the second is just well-organised guesswork.

Identify the Right Options

While clarity around questions is a great start, it's equally important to get to a solid set of options or, if some decisions are binary — hypotheses. The major challenge that many organisations come across is to push on with the default option or solution that has gained momentum organically. Unlike merit-based assessment, organic drift often happens through advocacy of the vocal stakeholders, who may fall prey to the sunk cost bias.

Let's expand the consent platform case study from chapter 8. Imagine the team had jumped straight to options without framing the right problem first. They might have come up with something like this:

— Option 1: Do nothing — leaves the business exposed due to recent regulatory changes, lifting risk above appetite.
— Option 2: Implement the recommended vendor platform through a multi-year, multi-million-dollar program.
— Option 3: Build a bespoke platform in-house — twice as long, three times the cost.

Looks like analysis, doesn't it? Except Options 1 and 3 are dummies. Both clearly fail the constraints around compliance, timeline, or cost. They exist only to make Option 2 look reasonable.

The real options could include (in the order of complexity and cost):

— Option 1: Implement only customer-facing updates (user experience and communications) to ensure compliance with the regulatory change.
— Option 2: Implement customer-facing updates and minor back-end tweaks leveraging existing technology stack to ensure compliance and minimise operational risk.
— Option 3: Implement the recommended vendor platform through a multi-year multi-million-dollar program to future-proof solution for any future regulatory changes and use cases (if they arise).

Now, these options can be properly costed and evaluated on their merit. With the right options in place, what has been the "default" recommendation may no longer look like an obvious choice.

Some questions, particularly when they are more binary in nature, may be better suited to be tackled as hypotheses that need to be tested rather than a set of options from which to select. In the example above, the binary version of the decision could be around whether the business needs to implement a standalone consent management platform (vs can achieve its objectives with the tweaks to the existing systems).

The simplest approach to setting the hypothesis is to look at the objectives and key results and pick the one that aligns best. If the business prioritises the KRs around keeping the cost of compliance within the current budget (which would make a standalone platform difficult) it would likely start with a hypothesis that the existing systems with some tweaks could do the job. If the primary focus was on maximum flexibility and future-proofing, the starting hypothesis could be that the new platform is required, unless proven otherwise.

It would work the other way around as well. What's most important is not where you start, but how sincerely you test those hypotheses. If the team is doing a box-ticking exercise aiming to support their existing position, no matter which way you start, you'll end up with a predetermined answer. To get to the "right answer" the team needs to be open-minded and willing to prove itself wrong if the evidence points that way.

One of the key pitfalls is developing compromise options — what I call «Frankensteins». Sometimes those hybrid options work, but if you hear "could we have a bit of A and a bit of B" where A and B are the opposites or completely incompatible — beware. When situations like this come up, the root cause is often far deeper than the choice at hand. Whether it's mere unwillingness to change one's mind, fear of losing face, misaligned incentives, "turf protection" or something else — instead of wrestling your way through it, invest effort in getting to the core and try to discreetly address it.

Real options table

The simple yet super powerful tool in decision-making is what I call "real options table". In fact, it is so good, I have not yet come across a problem I couldn't work through using it.

As we discussed above, all the options that you put forward must be real and debatable, not dummies that everyone would discard.

The options ideally should differ across one dimension rather than varying across a set of dimensions. However, blended or composite options also work in certain circumstances as we'll see below.

Let's take an example of an insurance company evaluating employee benefit options that it can offer to staff on its own products. There may be multiple dimensions of benefits such as the level of staff discount (e.g. 10%, 20% or 30%), products to which the discount applies (e.g. home, pet, car and life insurance), and the extension of access to family members of employees.

One approach could be to blend all three aspects in a composite option — e.g.

- Conservative — 10% off on travel, pet and life insurance, excluding family members.
- Medium — 20% off on travel, pet and life insurance, 10% off car insurance, excluding family members.
- Generous — 30% off on all products, also available to all family members.

Another approach would be to have options with pros and cons across each dimension — i.e. one table per dimension:

- Level of discounts: 10%, 20%, and 30%.
- Eligible products: home, pet, car, and life insurance.
- Family member coverage: included vs not included.

The most comprehensive one would be to have a three-dimensional matrix, where for each product you evaluate the level of discount and family inclusion. That approach would yield 3 (discounts) x 4 (products) x 2 (family inclusion options) = 24 permutations. Indeed, that's a lot of optionality!

Sometimes the extra level of detail is helpful, sometimes it's overkill. For instance, if there's a budget or other constraint limiting the flexibility, composite options could work well. Looking back at our example: if the only way to offer a 30% discount is to exclude low margin car insurance and family members, then blending three dimensions is preferable.

The real options table consists of four swim-lanes:

1) Description: Each option needs to be described across the critical aspects that make it distinct from others. It's best to avoid blurry lines and overlaps as much as possible. Often an overlap or blurriness between options indicates that there's a dimension that may require its own options table. The description may also include quantitative parameters, such as cost, duration, resource requirements of the option.

2 and 3) Pros and cons: Each option should have its pros and cons. Aim to make these concise. Where relevant, back the argument for or against a certain option with quantitative data such as dollars, sprints, transaction volumes, or FTEs. Risks (such as implementation or operational) would often fit within "CONS" swim-lane. Potential downstream or longer-term opportunities that the option opens up fit well alongside "PROS".

4) WYNTB: Last, but not least is "What you need to believe" (WYNTB) swim-lane. This is a punchline that boils down the option to the key assumption that would make it the best choice. In our employee benefit example, the WYNTB for the generous option could be "despite negative net margin on sales to staff and their families, maximising uptake of company products will improve advocacy among employees and lead to a material uplift in sales performance". For the least generous, WYNTB could be something like "discounts above 10% may undermine employee perception of the premium status and exclusivity of access to our products".

FIGURE 9.1: REAL OPTIONS TABLE TEMPLATE

	Option 1	Option 2	Option 3	Option 4
Option description				
Pros				
Cons				
What you need to believe				

The number of options to consider will vary from question to question. Two to four usually works best. If you are getting more than four, it may indicate that you are trying to cram multiple questions or decisions into one. Break it up, and analysis (discussed further) will be more straightforward.

To bring this approach to life, let's use a staff discount example introduced earlier.

FIGURE 9.2: REAL OPTIONS TABLE EXAMPLE

	Conservative	Medium	Most generous
Option description	10% off on travel, pet and life, excluding family members	20% off on travel, pet and life, 10% off car insurance, excluding family members	30% off on all products, also available to all family members
Pros	- low cost to the business - simpler to implement across only two product lines	- employee value proposition broadly in line with market - aligned with product margins	- category leading employee value proposition - high penetration and advocacy impact among staff and families - simple to communicate
Cons	- below-market employee value proposition - exclusion of car insurance may be negatively perceived - unlikely to drive internal take-up and advocacy	- more complex to communicate market parity of staff discounts is sufficient to retain employees and drive advocacy	- negative margins, particularly on car insurance, for staff and families
What you need to believe	discounts above 10% may undermine employee perception of the premium status and exclusivity of access to our products	market parity of staff discounts is sufficient to retain employees and drive advocacy	despite negative net margin on sales to staff and family members, maximising product uptake will improve internal advocacy and lead to a material uplift in the staff retention and sales performance

What you need to believe   discounts above 10% may undermine employee perception of the premium status and exclusivity of access to our products   market parity of staff discounts is sufficient to retain employees and drive advocacy   despite negative net margin on sales to staff and family members, maximising product uptake will improve internal advocacy and lead to a material uplift in the staff retention and sales performance

Once these real options are documented, it often becomes self-evident which way to lean. If you get to two or even three hotly contested options, where people disagree on which way to go, you've struck decision-making gold!

One of the shortest paths to resolution is to crystallise "What you need to believe" statements and shift the conversation to the level of conviction in those underlying beliefs being true. Sometimes it comes down to numbers and risk appetite. In other cases, it's a more philosophical question — a distinction we'll dig into later in this chapter.

Portfolio selection

Not every decision comes down to picking one option from a shortlist. Sometimes you're selecting a combination — a set of initiatives to fit a budget, a bundle of features for a new product, or a mix of benefits to include in a customer subscription. These are portfolio decisions, and they come with their own flavour of complexity.

If the portfolio can be optimised mathematically — say, a capital allocation problem where each initiative has a known cost, expected return and risk profile — there are quantitative tools for that. Linear programming, Monte Carlo simulations, NPV maximisation under constraints. Use them. This section is not about those.

This section is about the messier, more common variety: multi-dimensional portfolio choices where there's no formula that spits out the "right" answer. The kind where you're weighing qualitative factors, strategic alignment, stakeholder preferences, and gut feel — all at once. Without a structured approach, these decisions are prime candidates for analysis paralysis, circular conversations at the Steering Committees, and the dreaded "let's revisit next week" loop that never ends.

The approach is similar in spirit to the real options analysis above, but applied across a broader set of candidates. In most cases it works well in three steps.

Step 1: Compile the long list. Get everything on the table. Every initiative, feature, benefit, or idea that's been floated. Don't filter yet — just document. The goal is completeness, not quality. You want the team and external stakeholders to feel heard, and you want to make sure nothing consequential slips through the cracks. A simple one-liner per item with a brief description is generally sufficient at this stage.

Step 2: Filter out the chaff. This is where your OKRs, constraints and guiding principles earn their keep. For each item on the long list, ask three questions. Does it meaningfully progress at least one key result? Does it fit within the stated constraints? Is it consistent with the guiding principles? If the answer to any of these is a clear "no", it's out. Don't agonise over borderline cases yet — just remove the obvious non-starters. What you're left with is a shortlist of candidates that have earned the right to compete for a spot in the portfolio.

One thing to watch for during the filtering process is dependencies between candidates. Portfolio items are not always independent. Sometimes feature A only delivers value if feature B is also included. Other times, initiative X makes initiative Y redundant. Flag these linkages early. Even a simple note like "requires Y" or "supersedes Z" next to the item will do. Ignoring dependencies risks assembling a portfolio that looks coherent on the PowerPoint slide but unravels in practice, when the team discovers halfway through that a critical enabler was left below the line.

Step 3: Prioritise what moves the needle most. With a manageable shortlist in hand, assess each candidate's relative contribution to the objectives. This is where it gets subjective, and that's fine. Use the real options table format if it helps — pros, cons, and "what you need to believe" for each. Where two candidates seem equally compelling, go back to your guiding principles, particularly the top-ranked one. That's your tiebreaker. The output is an ordered list in which you can draw the line based on available budget, capacity or appetite.

To make evaluation easier, you may need to include some standardised dimensions in your pros or cons, e.g. low / mid / high complexity rating, cost or revenue bands, e.g. <$200k, $200-500k, >$500k. If you have two clear dimensions, e.g. scale vs gross margin or complexity vs impact, a simple plot diagram may help visually assemble a right portfolio to fit within the parameters, e.g. budget or estimated gross margin.

In most cases, the prioritised list where a thick line separates what's in and what's out needs to go through a couple of iterations to ensure nothing gets missed. Sometimes the line moves (e.g. extra budget gets allocated to fit a few additional essential elements), sometimes the items move (e.g. upon closer look a feature may turn out more complex to deliver and move down in the list).

Worth remembering that "what's in" and "what's first" are two separate decisions. Even after the portfolio is agreed, the order in which items are delivered can materially affect outcomes. A feature that de-risks three other items should probably go first, regardless of its standalone impact. Similarly, quick wins that build momentum and stakeholder confidence early can buy the team goodwill for the harder items later. Don't let sequencing happen by default. Give it some deliberate thought once the portfolio is locked.

One thing to keep in the back of your mind: resist the temptation to include everything that survived the filter. A portfolio stuffed with "good enough" items dilutes focus and stretches resources thin. It cannot be about pleasing everyone by including everyone's ideas in the final list. The 50:1 rule applies here too. A tight portfolio of a handful of high-impact choices will almost always outperform a bloated one.

Binary choices

For some decisions "yes" or "no" answer would be sufficient, so exploring of multiple options is an overkill. For those binary decisions, you can still use the simplified version of the real options table with just one column for the hypothesised choice.

Let's revisit our wellbeing rewards program design from chapter 7. Once the team had landed that they were going to build a currency-based program (i.e. using points to reward healthy behaviours), they had to make a difficult choice around platform architecture. The going-in hypothesis was that the wellbeing platform (the one that tracks activities, goals and challenges) will be sufficient to manage points rewards as well. However, a technical due diligence disproved that hypothesis, and showed that the wellbeing platform was unable to fulfil all the requirements. So, they had to set up another work-stream to select a rewards platform for the points ledger and rewards catalogue.

The danger with binary choices is the potential for bias towards the default hypothesis. It's certainly a matter of personal preference, but one of the good ways to overcome the bias is to switch default hypotheses around. Instead of coming in with a base case that the wellbeing platform can handle everything they need, the team could start off with an opposite hypothesis that the existing platform is insufficient and try to prove themselves wrong. Regardless of where you start, there needs to be genuine curiosity and desire to get to the right answer, not to prove that your view is right.

The Dangers of the Preferred Hypothesis Bias

An investor-backed start-up was eager to disrupt allied health payments (for services such as dental, optical, or physio) in Australia.

Their going-in hypothesis was the all-too-common "allied health payments market is ripe for disruption". The second hypothesis was that "we have a brilliant tech solution that worked well in the hospitality sector overseas". The business choice they were making off the back of those was to invest in building a similar solution for the Australian healthcare sector.

In their mind it was a perfect product-market fit. In reality, the proverbial hammer was in a desperate search of nails.

The start-up approached a couple of major health funds with a partnership pitch. Well-articulated packs painting a grim picture of the current state of health payments lacked one thing — reality.

In the real world the customers didn't experience problems with claiming. An incumbent player controlled about 95% of electronic allied claims. Most funds offered claiming via their mobile apps. The paper claims were declining at a rapid pace representing only a small fraction of the total volume.

After getting some less than enthusiastic responses from the industry, the founders weren't prepared to give up on their hypotheses. Instead, they tried to salvage the pitch by shifting the narrative from "the experience is terrible, we'll fix it" to "the quasi monopoly is bad, we'll beat it".

Again, it lacked grounding in reality as the incumbent was only making a modest profit. For them it was a customer relationship play rather than a profit generating product! Capturing a few percentage points of market share would not have made any money for the start-up.

Still persistent they tried to pitch how they could start with those couple of percentage points (not making money) and then broaden into adjacencies like Medicare, National Disability Insurance Scheme, and Workers' Compensations Schemes. What they struggled to realise is that standing up a three-way marketplace (with tens of thousands of providers, dozens of funders and millions of customers) is mission impossible unless you have a head start of at least one — or preferably two — sides sorted.

The founders were deflated: their hypotheses were busted and the business choice was not looking realistic. The health payments market was clearly not ripe for disruption, at least not in the way they thought. Their solution was also not suitable in the healthcare context.

Giving up on what seemed like a brilliant start-up idea was hard, but it saved them millions of dollars and years of life!

Analysis: Philosophical vs Analytical Problems

In your decision-making journey you would have likely come across two broad types of questions. With the first type, let's call it "analytical", we can rely on a quantitative or logical analysis. The second type is often trickier and requires some soul searching, going back to enterprise values or guiding principles — let's call it "philosophical".

Analytical questions are more straightforward. To illustrate those, we can go back to our wellbeing rewards program example. One of the questions is around how much value to invest in rewards based on the expected returns. While complex, this challenge can be cracked analytically with some degree of confidence. An economic model of the program would take into account run costs, costs of rewards as well as the expected benefits. Then based on how much return the business requires the team will find an equilibrium level of rewards per member. As with any forecast of that nature, the answer is guaranteed to be wrong. Both cost and benefit assumptions will have a high degree of uncertainty yielding an imperfect estimate. Nonetheless, this best estimate is probably going to be within the ballpark and is certainly way better than having no estimate at all.

Analytical questions can involve selection of an option based on quantitative or logical assessment. In our example above, the business may consider low, medium and generous rewards options. The real options table would outline the expected costs and benefits of each and WYNTB could boil it down to the level of confidence in underlying assumptions. The decision could come down to investment capacity and risk appetite. If the stakeholders are bullish (prepared to take risk) and have budget to invest, they may lean towards a more generous option from the get-go. Conversely, they may bias to a "low" option if they are confident in customer appeal even with conservative level of rewards, but need to prove the case to unlock budgets before accelerating scale-up.

Philosophical questions are generally harder to crack. An example of a philosophical question is which partners to bring into the coalition. One option is to stick to health and wellbeing brands (e.g. sport apparel, wearables, gyms, healthy nutrition, pharmacies). The other approach could be to expand it to wellbeing-adjacent lifestyle brands (e.g. adding leisure travel, spa centres, orthopaedic bedding). Finally, there's an option to make it unconstrained (e.g. cinema tickets, fuel vouchers, or mobile phone plans). There are certainly commercial implications of each approach. The broader the coalition, the more engagement and liquidity the program would expect. However, this issue is hard to tackle purely analytically. It's more of a "could we vs should we" discussion. How comfortable are we expanding to lifestyle? Does it still align with our guiding principle of "in service of customer health"? Should we reconsider the guiding principle to drive growth through the unconstrained partner coalition?

The choices for those philosophical questions can be explored through the same real options table, but the discussion would usually centre around guiding principles, or even higher order guidelines such as enterprise mission, vision and values.

Imagine a company exploring an opportunity to capture sensitive customer health data that is related to the service that is provided as part of an existing platform integration project. In the future such data can be used to identify health needs and personalise experiences, however, in the near to medium term there's no capacity to make use of it. On the surface, it may seem sensible to capture additional data in the data warehouse now and develop use cases for it later. However, if the enterprise operates with a principle that they only capture and use customer health data when it is of benefit to the customer, the answer becomes a resounding no.

A word of caution for the world where analytical tools are becoming incredibly powerful. AI can now produce detailed scenario models, ranked option lists and confidence intervals in a fraction of the time it used to take a team of analysts. That is useful, especially for the analytical questions we discussed above. But it's not without a risk. Leaders can be seduced into treating AI's clean and compelling analytical outputs as the answer rather than an input to the conversation. The question you framed, the assumptions you baked in, the context you fed it, all of that determines what comes out the other end. The philosophical questions, the ones that require going back to values and guiding principles, are where human judgement matters most. Don't let the polish of the output trick you into skipping the thinking and a good debate.

Think a Few Steps Ahead

In complex decisions where multiple parties are involved, the team may need to think several steps ahead and consider potential downstream impacts and consequences. If a company is choosing how aggressive to discount their products during sale, they may need to consider potential moves of their competitors and subsequent response.

Without trying to cram a game theory book in this section, let's discuss just one very basic tool to support option analysis — decision trees and tables.

Take a retail brand considering what level of discounts to offer for Black Friday. The market benchmark historically has been 30%. They expect that major competitors will stick to that approach. However, the company needs to catch up on the market share which has been slowly declining, and Black Friday could be an opportunity to close the gap and finish the year strong. The option they may consider running is an ultra-aggressive 50% off for 3 days or for two weeks prior to Black Friday to capture significantly more sales.

The challenge is if its major competitors follow suit — all end up with losses. The only way this campaign can pay off if the company is the only one doing it. An unrivalled two-week campaign would pay off big time — landing everyone a good end-of-year bonus. A three-day unrivalled campaign would just get them back on plan. The risk of discount matching of a two-week campaign is high, for a 3-day campaign — it's estimated to be low as there's not much time for the competitors to respond. Going in with their default 30% discount will land the company under plan, but it won't get the team fired. If, in the unlikely event, a major competitor went ahead with 50% off first, the company would be in a lot of trouble.

This complex campaign decision can be broken down into a decision tree or a matrix and analysed based on the estimated likelihood and outcome of plausible scenarios. It's often impossible to scientifically estimate probabilities and outcomes, but the teams grappling with such problems can use historical proxies, industry benchmarks and their best judgement. A well thought through decision is always better than a wild guess.

Without diving into the depth of game theory a number of insights emerge from the analysis. There are only four plausible scenarios that we need to consider — the remaining five scenarios are unlikely or not applicable. Going with 50% off for two weeks is highly likely to lead to a commercial disaster when rivals respond. Keeping 30% is the safest option, which with a decent level of confidence lands the company under plan for sales. Going in with a medium-risk 50% for 3 days has a decent chance of allowing the company to hit the plan despite the margin hit. If, however, competitors are prepared and respond rapidly (which is possible), not only the company will miss the sales target, but will also take a major margin hit.

FIGURE 9.3: DECISION MATRIX EXAMPLE

	Keep 30%	50% for 3 days	50% for two weeks
Rivals go first with 50%	Likehood: **Highly unlikely** Outcome: **Badly miss sales plan**	N/A	Likehood: **Highly unlikely** Outcome: **Disaster** — sales and profit badly impacted
Rivals respond with 50%	N/A	Likehood: **1/3 probability** Outcome: **Miss plan, take profit hit**	Likehood: **Highly likely** Outcome: **Disaster** — sales and profit badly impacted
Rivals do not respond (keep 30%)	Likehood: **Likely** Outcome: **Miss sales plan**	Likehood: **2/3 probability** Outcome: **Exceed plan** — with volumes offsetting margin loss	Likehood: **Unlikely** Outcome: **Significantly exceed sales plan,** get bonuses

Shaded cells — indicate plausible scenarios

Sometimes the choice is straightforward when scenarios yield significantly different payoffs. In many cases, though, it boils down to the relative importance of OKRs that the decision is impacting. That's where prioritisation of OKRs (and guiding principles) comes to the fore. If this company's No.1 objective is market share growth and KRs are biased towards sales rather than profit, it may go with the medium-risk 50% for 3 days option. If the company is less concerned about market share, but has low tolerance to profit impact, it will probably choose the safest default 30% option.

The example we discussed above is a relatively straightforward one. In real life, companies often face more complex multi-step decisions, but almost all of those can be simplified and broken down into manageable chunks. I am yet to come across a decision that this approach, admittedly with some bashing into shape, couldn't crack.

Make Recommendations

The first rule when it comes to making recommendations is not to be on the fence. If you've got your choices worked through, there should be only one that gets put forward for discussion and final decision. Not everyone may agree with it. The recommended option may not end up being the chosen one. But the team can't start a debate while on the fence.

For major decisions, if there are strong divergent views on which option to put forward even within the team, the team leader can make the initial call. But where strong divergent views emerge, this is an indication that a broader forum (including a few HIPPOs) may be required to ensure the business is making the right call and everyone gets on board.

The second rule is to keep it as simple as possible. When it comes to recommendations, complexity is evil. Unfortunately, the simplest recommendations are often the hardest to make. A simple way is almost always uphill — it takes courage and effort. If it took the team a lot of time and deep thinking to land the answer, there'll always be a temptation to demonstrate how complex the journey was. Resist the urge. Take or give credit for the hard work without complicating the recommendation.

For those who remember pre-cloud days, file sharing across multiple PCs was at best cumbersome: SFTP servers, shared drives, emails and floppy disks (now, I'm showing my age). In came Dropbox and solved it by adding a cloud folder to our desktop. Behind this ultimate simplicity was an incredibly sophisticated (for those times) piece of technology which took months of hard work to develop. Users didn't care how much effort it took, but they loved the experience and embraced it in big numbers.

As we've seen with the options, a common way to complicate recommendations is to "Frankenstein" them. We discussed that sometimes there's scope for taking the best parts of a couple of options and voilà — you've got a best-of-both-worlds solution. But in many cases, if the options have been well thought through and "hybridisation" is not helpful, it could be a sign of stakeholders seeking a suboptimal but ego-friendly compromise.

Before advancing to the debate and commitment step it's helpful to have a close look at your recommendation. If it's not crystal clear (recall our discussion on clarity in chapter 7), consider going back a step and revisiting the options.

Debate and Commit

We discussed the importance of having the right conditions (FOCS) for decision-making in the previous chapter. The most important underlying prerequisite for a constructive debate is openness which relies on trust. If you want high-quality and high-pace decision-making — invest heavily in trust within the team and across business units and build a habit of open, respectful and constructive discussions.

Develop the environment where everyone is comfortable challenging each other and voicing divergent views. Listen to the quiet resistance and invite people to share concerns, however small they may seem. Sometimes there are barely visible risks or show-stoppers, which people may struggle to articulate and choose to withhold. The more consequential the decision is, the more important it is to reveal those subtle concerns.

Amazon's "Have Backbone; Disagree and Commit"

Amazon is probably the best-known exemplar of encouraging healthy debates and then ensuring firm commitment even if disagreement persists. It's a simple idea that many organisations say they want but rarely tolerate in practice. Leaders and team members are expected to challenge decisions when they disagree, even when it's uncomfortable, even when the idea came from someone senior.

Amazon codified this in its leadership principles as "Have Backbone; Disagree and Commit". People are expected to challenge vigorously — without softening their views or sugar-coating just to preserve harmony. But once the decision is made, everyone is expected to commit fully, even if they still disagree.

This combination of open challenge before the decision and real commitment after it solves a common organisational failure where teams either avoid disagreement (to stay "aligned") or keep disagreeing and relitigating after the call is made (to protect ego). At Amazon, debate is encouraged for a purpose: to reveal the best arguments and risks early, while there's still time to change course.

Jeff Bezos gave a practical example in a shareholder letter: a team wanted to proceed with a direction he didn't personally agree with. Instead of forcing them into prolonged persuasion cycles, he responded with "I disagree and commit", backing the team to run with the decision and calling out how much slower the organisation would have been if they had to win him over rather than secure his commitment.

Importantly, this principle does not imply that the decisions must "always move fast". It's all about separating the steps. In the debate step, the organisation must make it safe and expected for all team members to challenge assumptions, bring data, and argue the case. In the commit step, the teams must eliminate any ambiguity: one decision, one direction, one execution plan. Truth is allowed in the room, and once the call is made, the organisation moves as one.

We've already touched a couple of times on the role of HIPPOs, senior executives with delegation of authority. On high-stakes decisions you want to bring the key senior leaders into the room to hear the conversation and accept or, in exceptional circumstances, override the recommendations. On the less consequential ones, you can invite them to the showcase, where the options and choices get presented more for feedback, without the need for a formal endorsement.

A well set-up system relies on the teams in charge of the bulk of decision-making. In an ideal world, the role of HIPPOs is to provide guidance and oversight, and ensure cross-business alignment. As they typically carry the formal enterprise delegation, they are legally responsible for the decisions and have full authority to veto and override. And as with any effective system, leaders' veto rights and ability to override should only be used as a last resort.

Netflix's Context Over Control

Netflix built its decision culture around the premise that good decisions happen when responsible people are given context, not control. Rather than finessing the proverbial RACIs and routing choices through layers of approvals, Netflix emphasises pushing decisions down, so long as teams have clarity on the mission, strategy, and trade-offs. The culture memo talks about building "decision-making muscles at every level", and notes that Netflix prides itself on how few decisions senior leaders make.

That model only works if debate is healthy. If teams are expected to decide, they must be able to challenge each other's thinking and present concerns early without waiting for a senior to "step in". Netflix's approach leans heavily on information sharing (broad internal transparency) and direct dialogue, including mechanisms like internal memos where people can comment and ask questions.

This matters because the fastest way to create bad autonomy is to give people freedom without shared context — you get fragmentation and local optimisation. Netflix tries to avoid that by fostering alignment on destination and constraints, then letting teams choose the best pathway.

Practically, this shows up as a strong bias to debate the "why" and "what" (the intent, outcomes, and guardrails) while leaving the "how" to the team closest to the work. Managers are expected to provide the context that makes decisions easier, rather than becoming the bottleneck that makes decisions slower.

A well-known decision-making productivity killer is the phrase, "Let's circle back offline before we commit". When it comes up, first of all, ensure that everyone is clear on the concern that is being raised. There's no harm in asking clarifying questions and repeating it back. Once the concern is clear, there are two potential pathways:

— The faster and more efficient one is to collectively endorse the decision subject to validating concern. It could sound something like "The team will explore these issues over the next couple of days to see if there are red flags. Unless there's a showstopper, we'll progress with the recommended approach. Otherwise, we'll come back to this group with an alternative."

— The other more onerous option is to agree on the steps to validation, timelines and responsible stakeholders, and defer the formal commitment to the later forum (or offline approval process).

At the end of the decision-making meeting, whatever the format is, there should be an explicit commitment on a specific recommendation (or next steps with timelines and responsible stakeholders for getting to it). Make it so clear that there's no space for misinterpretation.

On the big consequential decisions, it helps to outline all the considerations that were debated and risks raised. With the modern AI scribing tools creating meeting minutes has become a lot easier, and it can save a lot of headache and memory blackouts down the line.

The bottom line is — commit collectively and explicitly even if some stakeholders are still uncomfortable. The ability to disagree and then genuinely commit is a sign of good decision-making discipline.

Execute and Pivot If Circumstances Change

You may wonder why 'execution' has crept into a decision-making book. Fair challenge. However, there are a couple of things that we need to unpack to ensure that the choices deliver results rather than become intellectual gymnastics.

The first point is that there should be mechanisms in place to ensure that the decisions get implemented correctly. We've all come across situations where the team or multiple teams responsible for implementation take a lot of creative licence and steer way off the intended path. It often happens when the teams responsible for strategy and design choices are different from those who deliver. The most sensible approach that is the hardest to implement is to set up end-to-end teams responsible for everything from strategy and design to delivery and operations.

Spotify Squads and End-to-End Ownership

Spotify became well known for its "squad" model. The model was not new, but Spotify took it to the next level, making it brutally practical for high-quality decision-making, execution, and rapid pivoting.

A Spotify squad is a small, autonomous, cross-functional team, typically six to eight people. The team is designed to be small enough to move fast, but large enough to get meaningful work done without complex dependencies.

Each squad owns a clearly defined product or customer problem end-to-end. A typical squad includes:
— *a Product Manager, accountable for outcomes and priorities;*
— *several Software Engineers, responsible for building and maintaining the solution;*
— *a Designer, ensuring usability and customer experience; and*
— *often access to Data/Analytics and QA, embedded or tightly aligned.*

Crucially, these squads are not delivery factories executing someone else's decisions. They are expected to make decisions, ship changes, observe real customer behaviour, and adjust accordingly. The same team that debates a solution is responsible for building it, operating it, and living with the consequences. This eliminates a common failure in large organisations where intent is lost in handoffs between strategy, design, delivery, and operations.

Squads are grouped into tribes (collections of squads working on related areas), which provide alignment and shared direction without removing autonomy. The role of leadership is to set context, including strategy, priorities, and guardrails. The senior leaders deliberately refrain from micromanaging. If circumstances change, squads don't need to escalate for permission to pivot; they already have the authority and capability to do so.

The quality and pace of execution improve when decision rights and delivery capability sit in the same place. Spotify's model doesn't prevent mistakes, but it ensures that mistakes are promptly identified, clearly owned, and quickly corrected.

Where implementation of an end-to-end model is impossible or impractical, the strong alignment between upstream and downstream teams is paramount. All critical stakeholders or at the very least the leadership of key downstream teams should be closely involved in the decision-making process. The earlier they get "on the bus", the better. You'll almost certainly run into trouble if they aren't involved by the debate-and-commit stage.

The second pitfall to avoid is relitigating committed decisions at all costs. Properly debated choices are less prone to it, but are not immune. Sometimes there's a strong urge to "revisit" the choices despite the commitment due to some residual discomfort. That's not a good excuse.

However, there are situations where a pivot is justified. The litmus test is, "Has new evidence emerged, or have the circumstances changed to an extent that it may change the answer?" If so — reopen the decision and consider pivot options. If not — stay the course.

No Decision Is Still a Decision

In 2008, a major superannuation administrator managing millions of pension accounts set out to rebuild its core platform from scratch. The new platform was designed as an all-in-one powerhouse covering everything from superannuation administration and handling life and income protection insurance products to claims management.

At the time, a significant portion of contribution advices (instructions on how to allocate employer superannuation payments to individual accounts) arrived on paper. So, one of the platform's flagship features was a world-class paper processing and Optical Character Recognition (OCR) engine capable of reading any paper document, even hand-written forms, and processing them without human touch.

The scope was vast, and with limited delivery experience, the project suffered delay after delay. Budgets blew out from $70 million to around $250-300 million.

By 2013 — five years in — an industry shift had transformed the environment. Paper contribution advices were rapidly disappearing, replaced by electronic submissions. The government was about to mandate a digital-only standard.

The "world-class" OCR capability was no longer a strategic differentiator — it was becoming a relic.

And yet, the company kept building it.

No one stopped to ask: Do we still need this? Is this still the right investment? Requirements were never revisited. The project continued, full steam ahead, solving a problem that has all but disappeared.

In 2014, the company was sold to a competitor with a more modern, fit-for-purpose platform. It took a change of management to finally admit that investment in the OCR capability was a write-off. It was an expensive lesson about the danger of "deciding" by doing nothing, when circumstances require a painful pivot.

A sharp-eyed reader will notice that this chapter ends at the point of commitment and early execution. What about monitoring outcomes? Tracking whether the decision actually delivered what it was supposed to? Adjusting course based on real-world results? These are critical questions and I don't want to leave the impression that they don't matter — they absolutely do.

A decision without a feedback loop is a bet without a scoreboard. The discipline of defining objectives and success metrics upfront, tracking them through implementation, and honestly evaluating outcomes against expectations is what separates organisations that learn from those that repeat the same mistakes over and over. But covering that end-to-end lifecycle properly would take us deep into execution and operational territory, which deserves a separate book.

The promise was to stay focused and on point, and I intend to keep it. That said, if you want to explore the full decision-to-execution feedback loop, two frameworks are worth exploring. The first is the OODA loop — Observe, Orient, Decide, Act — which we mentioned in Chapter 5, developed by military strategist Colonel John Boyd. The second is the PDCA cycle — Plan, Do, Check, Act — a staple of continuous improvement since W. Edwards Deming popularised it in the 1950s.

Where OODA is built for speed and adaptation under uncertainty, PDCA is built for disciplined iteration and quality control. Eric Ries' «The Lean Startup» applies PDCA thinking to product and business model decisions through the Build-Measure-Learn loop. Both frameworks pick up where this book deliberately leaves off.

You now have the full toolkit for cracking individual decisions: real options, «what you need to believe», structured analysis, clear recommendations, healthy debate, firm commitment, and the discipline to pivot only when evidence demands it. Used well, this method will land you on the right answer most of the time — and at the very least, it'll surface the real disagreements early rather than after the deal is done.

But what happens when you're not facing one decision, but hundred — each shaping the others, with no clear starting point? That's the territory chapter 10 explores: complex, interdependent decision environments where the standard method needs to flex, and where capital budgeting becomes either a strategic weapon or a slow-motion disaster.

Chapter 10:
Decisions in Complex Systems

"Everything should be made as simple as possible, but not simpler."

— ALBERT EINSTEIN

The approach we've covered in chapters 8 and 9 works well for individual decisions — even highly complex ones. Define the objectives, set the constraints, frame the questions, develop real options, analyse, recommend, debate, commit, execute. Clean and linear.

But the real world isn't always that simple. In large-scale transformations, new product builds, market entries, and organisational redesigns, you rarely face one decision at a time. You face dozens — sometimes hundreds — of interconnected choices, where every answer can reshape the question set for everything else. Target customer affects value proposition. Value proposition affects operating model. Operating model affects cost structure. Cost structure affects pricing. Pricing affects target customer. Welcome to projects with infinite degrees of freedom, where the decision space is so vast and intertwined that the tools from the previous chapters, while essential, may not be sufficient.

Faced with this kind of complexity, most organisations either try to solve everything simultaneously or start making calls at random in the hope of stumbling upon a coherent set of answers. Neither works, so this chapter provides a practical method for navigating that middle ground.

The Decision Web

In a simple decision environment, the question is clear, options are bounded, and consequences are reasonably contained. You can often work through the decision linearly: frame the problem, develop options, analyse, recommend, decide. But projects with unconstrained optionality don't afford you that luxury.

Consider designing a new business from scratch. Target customer, value proposition, pricing, operating model, cost structure, technology, team design, go-to-market — each of these involves dozens of choices, and none of them are independent. Your target customer shapes your value proposition. Your value proposition dictates your operating model. Your operating model drives your cost structure. Your cost structure constrains your pricing. And your pricing determines which customers you can viably target. You're back where you started.

This is the chicken-and-egg problem of complex decision-making. Decision A depends on the answer to decision B, but B depends on A. When these circular dependencies multiply across a project, the whole system can freeze. Everyone waits for input from everyone else, meetings proliferate, but the progress stalls. Ever seen a frozen computer when the processor goes into overdrive, where the fans are spinning frantically but nothing is happening? The complex intertwined decisions can put an organisation into a similar deadlock — lots of activity with no movement.

Now layer on the volume. If your project involves just ten interconnected decisions with five plausible options each, you're looking at roughly 10 million possible combinations. You cannot possibly evaluate them all. You cannot spreadsheet your way out of it. And you certainly can't hold it all in your head during a two-hour Steering Committee.

Disney+: Infinite Degrees of Freedom in Action

When Disney was deciding whether to launch its own streaming platform in 2017-2018, the strategic logic was straightforward: own the customer relationship, stop licensing crown jewels to competitors, and build a direct-to-consumer business around the most recognisable content library on the planet. As a boardroom narrative it's rather simple, but the execution was a textbook project with infinite degrees of freedom.

Every major decision depended on several others. Content strategy questions such as what to pull from theatrical windows, what to produce exclusively, what to claw back from Netflix couldn't be finalised without a pricing model. But pricing depended on subscriber projections. Subscriber projections depended on how content appeal and market positioning convert into actual take-up and retention. Market positioning depended on the bundle strategy with Hulu and ESPN+. The bundle strategy depended on how aggressively Disney was willing to cannibalise its existing revenue streams. We are talking big dollars at stake — over $1.75 billion in annual sales of home entertainment (mostly via physical media such as DVDs) alone. And the appetite for cannibalisation depended on how quickly the platform revenues could scale to offset the losses, which brings us right back to content and pricing.

Then there were the operational dimensions. Technology platform, international rollout sequencing, partnership deals (Verizon offered a free year of Disney+ to its unlimited data customers, which is a pricing and volume decision rolled into one), content production pipeline, and the small matter of completing a $71 billion acquisition of 21st Century Fox's entertainment assets in parallel.

A linear step-by-step approach a-la "let's first decide on content, then pricing, then distribution" would have taken a long time costing them billions in expenses and forgone revenue. A free-for-all approach where "everyone just starts building" whatever they feel is best would have produced contradictions and rework at scale.

What Disney needed was a way to make high-consequence calls early, let those create structure for downstream decisions, and iterate when things didn't fit. That's the essence of what we'll cover in this chapter.

The natural human response to this kind of complexity is to gravitate toward one of two ends of the spectrum. One extreme is to try to boil the ocean by mapping every single dependency, modelling every permutation, refusing to commit until the full picture is clear. This path leads to months of "discovery" that produces frameworks and walls covered in process maps but no decisions. Another extreme is to start making disparate calls haphazardly, expecting that the pieces will fit together eventually. This often leads to incoherent choices and the painful realisation, months into the work, that different workstreams have been building against incompatible sets of assumptions.

Both responses are understandable, but hardly helpful. What's needed is a structured method for making progress through complexity without losing coherence — a way to impose order on the chaos without pretending it isn't chaotic.

The Sudoku Method: Identify, Stratify, Solve, and Iterate

If you've ever played Sudoku, you'd know that staring at 81 empty cells can feel paralysing. But experienced players don't try to solve the whole grid at once. They scan for the most constrained cells — the ones where surrounding numbers have already eliminated most possibilities — and start there. Each solved cell creates new constraints, making neighbouring cells easier. And if something doesn't work three moves later, you backtrack and try a different number.

The same logic applies to navigating a decision web. You can't solve everything at once, and you can't solve things at random. You need to find the decisions that will unlock the most progress downstream, nail those first, and let them create structure for everything else.

There are four steps involved. The first two steps are about mapping the choices, the last two — about tackling those.

Step 1: Identify. Start by getting all the decisions that need to be made on the table. In complex projects, this is partly a collection exercise and partly a discovery exercise. As we discussed in chapters 8 and 9, it is important to get to the real questions and real options, including the ones that sit beneath the surface.

The collection part is relatively straightforward: work through the project scope, the workstreams, the key milestones, and capture every choice that is being discussed, debated, or deferred. Most teams do this reasonably well.

The discovery part is harder, because some of the most consequential decisions are the ones nobody is talking about. Sometimes they are assumed as given, sometimes they are just not obvious to anybody, sometimes they are avoided out of political sensitivity. These are the decisions that, left unidentified, can ambush the project later.

Brainstorming sessions with sticky notes are one effective way to expose what's hiding. The physical act of writing a decision on a note and putting it on a wall lowers the barrier compared to saying it out loud in a room full of stakeholders. But the real value comes from the questions the facilitator asks after the first wave of notes goes up. Three prompts tend to unlock what's missing:

1) What big choices have we not yet considered?
2) What choices could we be avoiding?
3) Are any of our assumptions actually choices in disguise?

That last one is particularly powerful.

Flushing those out before you start stratifying and solving will save you from building a carefully tiered decision tree on top of a foundation that was never examined.

One last thing, depending on how big and coherent the long list is, it may need some polish to make it workable. Don't try to make the list academically perfect — just clean it up: ensure you remove the duplicates, clean out (or politely park) trivial and superficial choices, and align the language of the questions.

Step 2: Stratify. Once the list is ready, classify each of the items into tiers based on three dimensions: how consequential the decision is, how reversible it is, and how many other decisions it constrains.

A practical way to do this is a four-tier model. Let's use a design of a rewards program, which we used as an example in a few spots before to bring the tiers to life.

You'll recognise the 50:1 principle at work here — concentrate your effort on the decisions that disproportionately determine the outcome.

The difference in a decision web is that tiering must also account for interdependencies: a Tier 1 decision isn't just consequential on its own —

FIGURE 10.1: THE DECISION TIERING FRAMEWORK

	Examples	Who typically decides
Tier 1 — The most fundamental, structural choices. High influence on downstream decisions, high consequence, hard to reverse.	Target customer definition, core proposition structure (e.g. are we building a currency-based vs status-based rewards program), business model fundamentals (e.g. capex, budget per user).	Group executives or board endorse (in line with corporate delegations) based on team recommendations.
Tier 2 — Highly consequential choices that underpin economics or design. Material downstream dependencies. Includes decisions involving above-medium risk.	Points expiry rules, rewards earn mechanics, major scoping decisions with significant cost or complexity implications, platform and vendor selection.	Accountable Senior Executive or Steering Committee endorses based on team recommendations.
Tier 3 — Significant design choices that are reversible in the short to medium term. Limited downstream dependencies. Medium or low risk.	Coalition partner commercial model (e.g. commissions vs points sales), breadth of partner portfolio, launch configuration of product features, program comms rules.	Team decides, ensuring the team lead is comfortable and making it visible to the Steering Committee and/or Accountable Senior Executive.
Tier 4 — Tactical and reversible decisions. No downstream dependencies. Below-medium risk.	Individual partner selection, launch campaign channels, media allocation, partner campaign configuration.	Team members decide autonomously, keeping the team lead informed.

it shapes the option set for dozens of decisions below it. The tiering serves two purposes. First, it focuses your most rigorous process on the decisions that warrant it. Tier 1 gets the comprehensive treatment, while Tier 4 choices can get away with just a real options table. Second, it sets clear governance expectations, so people know who makes the call and who needs to be in the room, which eliminates a significant number of circular conversations and second-guessing.

FIGURE 10.2: DECISION TREE: REWARDS PROGRAM DESIGN

Illustrative example of tiered decisions cascading from Tier 1 structural choices to Tier 4 tactical decisions

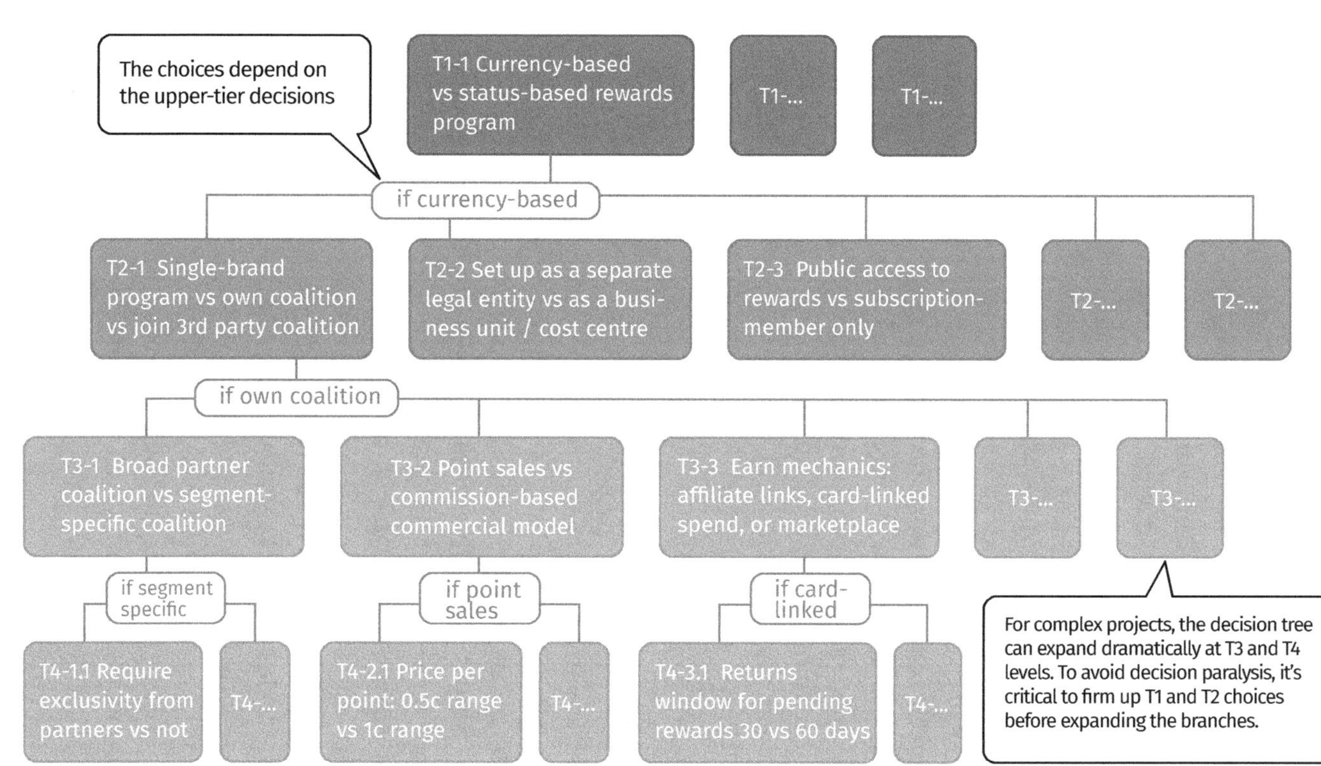

In the Disney+ example, content library strategy and pricing would sit squarely in Tier 1. Both were high-consequence (get either wrong and the platform fails), hard to reverse, and highly influential — almost every other decision depended on them. The Hulu/ESPN+ bundle structure would likely be Tier 2: consequential and with significant economic implications, but partially constrained once content and pricing were resolved. International rollout sequencing could sit at Tier 3: important but more reversible and less likely to break the whole model if adjusted later.

Once your decisions are tiered, it helps to map them visually as a decision tree — Tier 1 choices at the top, cascading down through Tiers 2, 3 and 4. Each branch represents that an upstream decision influences the choices below it. In our rewards program example (see the diagram), the Tier 1 choice of a currency-based program opens a branch of Tier 2 decisions around coalition model, legal setup and access eligibility, among other things. The downstream choices would have been quite different in a status-based model. The tree doesn't need to be perfectly mutually exclusive and collectively exhaustive (MECE in consulting-speak) to be useful. In a decision web, some downstream choices can sit under multiple upstream branches, and some relationships will be fuzzy. That's fine, because the value isn't in architectural perfection — it's in making the hierarchy of decisions and their dependencies visible, so everyone can see where they are, what's been resolved, what's outstanding, and what choices their past decisions can unlock.

Step 3: Solve from the top tiers down as best you can. Apply the toolkit from chapters 8 and 9 to your Tier 1 and Tier 2 decisions: define objectives, set constraints, frame questions, develop real options, analyse, recommend, debate, commit. It doesn't mean that you need to have a full stack of paperwork for every single choice. Usually, these decision tiers can be tackled as a package of interdependent choices (e.g. rewards program design) that would have a common frame (e.g. OKRs, constraints, guiding principles, exam questions).

Accept that they are going to be conviction-based bets, not certainties. You won't have perfect information and that's fine. A well-reasoned Tier 1 call at 70% confidence is infinitely more useful than no call aiming for 100% certainty.

A practical litmus test on which decisions to lean in earlier rather than later is to face into the ones that get you into the circular discussions most. If the choice itches — scratch it!

As part of this step, it's important to establish a discipline around documenting not just what was decided, but also why. The real options table framework from Chapter 9 is going to be your best friend here. The pros and cons, the "what you need to believe" assumptions, as well as minutes of the discussions held on the topic, including stakeholder feedback, will provide a robust base from which to move forward. This is definitely not bureaucracy for bureaucracy's sake. It's essential for good governance in complex environments where things can easily get lost or forgotten. When a downstream decision forces you to revisit a Tier 1 or Tier 2 call (and it occasionally will), you need to be able to trace what drove the original choice so you can reassess intelligently rather than starting from scratch.

From 40 Options to a 40-Foot Container

A mid-tier engineering company in Central Asia had built a solid business in fire security for the oil and gas sector. Revenue was stable, but the owners were growing uneasy. The bulk of earnings came from a couple of large projects. If one disappeared, the company would struggle. The long-term outlook after the major oilfield developments were completed was hazier still.

The founders wanted to diversify, and assembled a taskforce. The problem was that the opportunities were entirely unconstrained. The team could do anything from launching fire security operations in the Middle East to setting up a distribution business for new product categories across Central Asia to investing in property development. Conversations ran in circles, oscillating between different levels of detail and different opportunity branches in the same meeting. One moment the debate was about whether to enter a new geography; the next it was about whether to focus on premium or budget-grade products. Without a hierarchy of decisions, although discussions felt constructive, nothing was actually getting resolved.

The breakthrough came when the team started stratifying. They identified the Tier 1 choices: who are we selling to, what kind of products, and where? Each of those had to land before the downstream questions made any sense.

If the goal was to reduce dependency on a few large clients, they needed volume across many buyers. To build resilience against oilfield development cyclicality, they needed to look at faster-moving product categories, not equipment that lasts two decades. And they decided to play to their strengths by leveraging their existing office network rather than entering new geographies.

Within a few weeks, what had felt like an unwieldy universe of options collapsed into a focused plan: distribute personal protective equipment (PPE) across Central Asia, starting with a single showroom in the key oil town on the Caspian Sea. Build a distribution model that works in one high-potential location, then expand. Just two months later, the first 40-foot container, stacked to the roof with protective apparel, footwear, head protection, respirators, spill containment gear, and dozens of other product lines was dispatched to the company's newly built showroom.

The Sudoku Method in miniature. Once the Tier 1 choices landed, the Tier 2 and 3 decisions (launch location, channel model, and even the product range) fell into place almost naturally. The team just needed to stop debating everything at once and start solving from the top.

Step 4: Iterate. With Tier 1 and Tier 2 resolved, move to Tiers 3 and 4 of which there will be many! These decisions are now partially constrained by your upstream calls, which makes them more tractable. Work through them using the same toolkit, scaled appropriately.

The part that trips people up is when a Tier 3 decision hits a wall and the downstream implications don't work given an upstream assumption. You may recall a telehealth service example in Chapter 4, where an interpretation of regulatory restriction to providing a free trial service (Tier 3 choice) could have jeopardised the scale-up roadmap (Tier 2), putting the whole strategy (Tier 1) at risk. When this happens, you may have to go back to Tiers 1 and 2.

This isn't failure. This is the method working as designed. Like erasing a number in Sudoku when it breaks three rows down, revisiting a Tier 1 or Tier 2 call in light of new downstream evidence is a feature, not a bug. The key is to revisit with precision: which specific assumption broke, and what's the minimum upstream adjustment that fixes it? Ideally, you're not reopening the whole decision, but fine-tuning it.

The iterative nature of this process can be uncomfortable for some. It feels like indecision or going backwards, but it's not. This is actually the only honest way to navigate a system where you can't know everything upfront. The alternative is pretending that your first Tier 1 call is sacred and forcing all downstream decisions to contort around it, which is how organisations end up with mish-mash solutions that "fit" on paper but not in practice.

Sudoku of Capital Budgeting

One of the most common and probably most politically charged pieces of corporate decision-making is enterprise capital allocation. We are talking about the cross-business exercise where dozens of initiatives from different parts of the organisation compete for the same finite investment and resource pool. These initiatives span multiple business units, require shared resources, and can't be prioritised in isolation. If you've been through one, you'll know the pattern. Every business unit comes with a compelling (in their own view) list of asks. The sum of asks exceeds the budget by a factor of three, and the resulting negotiation is shaped in part by the formal process and in part by organisational politics.

Before diving into the mechanics, it's worth naming a deeper tension that frames the entire exercise. Companies operate between two ends of the spectrum when it comes to capital budgeting. One extreme, common among publicly traded companies, chases the numbers and biases decisions heavily towards hitting the next quarter's targets at the expense of longer-term capability building and future-proofing. The other extreme chases rainbows and unicorns, biasing heavily towards long-term opportunities, in the hope that short-term results will take care of themselves. The companies operate in between the two, gravitating towards one of the sides.

Neither posture is inherently right or wrong. But both can become dangerous when they go unexamined. This is an area where the board's guidance and direction can play a critical role in ensuring that the capital allocation posture reflects a deliberate strategic choice based on the risk appetite and growth ambition rather than an inherited reflex.

The core difficulty in capital portfolio decision-making is that the initiatives are not apples to apples. They deliver fundamentally different types of value — short-term cost savings versus long-term strategic flexibility, hard revenue versus risk mitigation, capability uplift versus regulatory compliance. And the costs are not just dollars. Closing underperforming retail stores carries political sensitivity. Displacing frontline staff with AI chatbots risks brand and employee perception damage. A four-day work week is cost-neutral only if the efficiency gains actually materialise. Often, trying to compare these costs and benefits quantitatively in a spreadsheet is an exercise in false precision.

The Sudoku method provides a way through. Let's walk through it using a hypothetical example of a financial services company. The illustrative portfolio is provided as a table at the end of this section.

Step 1. Identify. Start by getting every initiative on the table with a consistent set of dimensions such as rationale, estimated cost, timelines, expected value, delivery complexity, team involvement, links and interdependencies with other initiatives. The discovery prompts from Step 1 apply here too. Again, some of the most consequential initiatives could be the ones nobody has formally raised because they assumed the answer was obvious, or because they're politically inconvenient.

Where initiatives are difficult to compare purely on cost versus benefit — and they almost always are — it helps to agree on a couple of compound metrics that level the playing field.

The first is impact × conviction. Raw expected benefit or impact is easy to inflate. Weighting it by conviction forces a harder conversation: how confident are we that these benefits will materialise? A useful mental anchor is to think of conviction as a scale where 1.0 is "as certain as Apple announcing a new iPhone in September" and 0 is "as random as a bitcoin price movement". Critically, someone needs to own the impact figure and be prepared to stand behind it when it's time to report outcomes. High impact with low conviction is not a top portfolio priority — it's a hypothesis that needs more work.

The second is cost × risk. The base cost estimate should include all forms of costs with a reasonable contingency, not only direct incremental costs. For instance, it should consider an often-neglected opportunity cost of effort that staff and management will contribute instead of doing other things. Then the risk multiplier accounts for everything beyond that: delivery complexity, pipeline congestion, dependency on multiple vendors to deliver concurrently, political sensitivity. A straightforward initiative with a well-understood scope might sit at 1.0. A technically complex, cross-business effort with external vendor dependencies might warrant 1.5 or even higher.

Companies can use all manner of quasi-quantitative metrics to operationalise these — Harvey balls, star ratings, scales of 1 to 10. The mechanics matter less than the principle. In this simplified model, for an initiative to earn a chance above the line, its impact × conviction measure needs to offset, and ideally exceed, its cost × risk measure. This won't produce a mathematically precise answer, but it will certainly produce a robust conversation.

Step 2. Stratify. Initiatives naturally cluster into four layers, which work like tiers, but let's not call them that to avoid confusion.

The top three layers are the "big rocks" — material scale initiatives with tangible benefits and a reasonable level of conviction. These big rocks ensure the business can continue to operate, deliver commercial value and annual targets, and enable longer-term success.

The top layer is **compliance and high-risk mitigation** — adherence to regulatory changes, enforceable undertakings, legacy out-of-support platform migrations, incident remediations. These are the genuine must-haves, without which the business cannot continue. But beware: this category has strong gravitational pull. Teams quickly learn that labelling something "must-have" guarantees funding, so the boundary fades.

Leaders must hold the bar ruthlessly. If it's not genuinely a non-negotiable, it goes back into the competitive pool. A bloated must-have bucket is the fastest way to crowd out everything else.

The second layer of initiatives is around **commercial value delivery**. They are the ones that help hit this year's targets. Revenue growth, cost reduction, customer acquisition. These are the engine of the business case and usually the most fiercely contested, because every business unit believes theirs is the one that moves the needle most. This is where the impact × conviction lens is important. Projected millions in incremental revenue mean nothing if conviction is low and the person in charge of the Profit & Loss line is not prepared to own the number.

The third layer is **long-term enablement** — initiatives like platform upgrades, codebase modularisation or workforce capability development, which give business strategic flexibility or unlock future delivery speed and capacity but won't show returns this financial year. These are the easiest to deprioritise but dangerous to ignore. This is also where the short-term metrics versus long-term opportunity posture matters. An organisation that reflexively favours next-quarter results will systematically starve this bucket, compounding the cost of that neglect, which is rarely evident until it's too late. The organisation risks getting stuck in a perpetual cycle of patching and workarounds. Give these initiatives weight proportional to their long-term impact. If you don't, you'll be having the same conversation next year, except the "catch-up backlog" will be bigger and the cost higher.

The rest go into the fourth bucket. These are a mix of smaller initiatives (the "pebbles") and material-scale ones, where benefits or conviction is not sufficiently high. It's important to keep an eye on the trophy projects and low-conviction bets. These are the ones that sound exciting, but the expected impact is uncertain, the business case is soft, or the path to value is unclear. They may not necessarily be bad ideas. But they haven't yet earned a place above the line. Those deserve an honest conversation about finding a way to increase the expected value, increase conviction by validating the assumptions, or parking until the next cycle. Parking an initiative does not mean killing it — it's about respecting the discipline.

Step 3. Solve. Next look at the dependencies. Some things are best built together, e.g. a new product and the multi-product sales capability that supports it. Others must be sequenced, e.g. building and launching AI chatbots before rebuilding frontline workflows, not after, because the workflow design depends on what the bots can handle.

Based on the layering and dependencies, a priority order should emerge. The more downstream dependencies and the greater value the initiative has the higher it should sit on the list. The process of ordering must be as objective as possible, but it's nearly impossible to make it mathematically perfect. The perfection comes from discussion and constructive debate.

Once the ordering is done, draw the line. The dotted line is set based on available capital and team capacity (in our sample portfolio, it's $7.3 million). Everything above the line gets funded and resourced. But watch for bottlenecks — the constraint is not always money. If your digital squads are involved in nearly every initiative and one of them consumes half their capacity, you are at risk of overcommitting people before you run out of budget. Draw the line where teams can realistically deliver, not where the spreadsheet says the funding stops.

Below the dotted line, it's worth drawing a second solid line to identify the genuine runner-up initiatives that narrowly missed the cut and can be re-evaluated during the year if budget frees up or circumstances change. Everything below that line goes into the parking lot: ideas that are shelved until at least the next planning cycle. This distinction matters for governance: a runner-up has a path back, while the parked initiatives get a clear signal — not for now. Except, obviously, if circumstances change so dramatically that reassessment is justified.

Step 4. Iterate... and land. Once the initial portfolio is set, stress-test it, debate vigorously. Have you inflated the must-haves? Have you starved the long-term enablers? Are the dependencies properly accounted for and sequenced? Is there a capacity bottleneck that has been overlooked? Run it past the people who will actually do the work — they'll spot the conflicts that the steering committee won't.

Leveraging our focus principle from the "How" chapter: a tight portfolio of few, well-resourced initiatives will always outperform a bloated one where everything is chronically under-funded and under-resourced. When an initiative is borderline, default to «out» rather than «in» — we come back to this discipline with a concrete example in chapter 12.

FIGURE 10.3: ILLUSTRATIVE CAPITAL BUDGETING PORTFOLIO.

An illustrative portfolio of a fictional financial services organisation allocating ~$7.3 million of enterprise capital investment

Initiative	Duration, cost est.	Impact x confidence	Cost + effort x risk	Teams / bottlenecks	Dependencies		
Privacy reform compliance – update consent collection UX in line with new regulations	3 months / $200k	must do	●	Digital	N/A	Must do	Commit funding
Legacy payment platform migration to mitigate high risk related to out-of-support technology	3 months / $400k	must do	●●	Digital, finance	N/A	Must do	Commit funding
Upgrade identity management and onboarding UX to mitigate $6m pa of identity-related fraud	5 months / $700k	●●●●●	●●●	Digital, product, core platform	N/A	High-value	Commit funding
New insurance product development and launch to grow EBITDA by $3m pa in the premium segment	6 months / $1,500k	●●●●	●●●	Digital, product, core platform, marketing	Needs multi-product sales capability	High-value	Commit funding
Sales website rebuild to enable multi-product sales within one flow to drive $4m in EBITDA over 3 years	6 months / $1,200	●●●●	●●●●	Digital, product, core platform, marketing	Supports new product build	High-value	Commit funding
App and web code base modularisation to enable ~30% faster pace of parallel delivery across 4 digital squads	12 months / $2,500k	●●●	●●●	Digital, product, core platform, marketing	Takes out half of digi capacity per squad	Long-term enabler	Commit funding
AI chat-bot capability to handle basic service and sales queries (cost reduction target of $1,5m pa)	4 months / $800k	●●●	●●	Digital, core platform, enablement tech, data	Value unlock before frontline tools	Best to sequence	Commit funding
Frontline workflow rebuild to handle complex queries (cost reduction of $700k pa from year 2 and risk mitigation)	3 months / $400k	●●	●	Channels, product, core platform	Depends on launching AI bots	Best to sequence	Maybe
Brand relaunch campaign to grow awareness (incremental to base spend) – $2m EBITDA over 3 years	3 months / $2,000	●●	●●	Marketing, external relations	Value maximised post product launch		Maybe
Customer contact data remediation, including incentives for customers to update to improve comms efficiency and remove data gaps	9 months / $800k	●	●●	Digital, data, marketing	Lower impact if after AI chat-bot	Lower impact / confidence	Revisit next cycle
Migration to a new procurement platform to enable faster and more robust purchasing (improved staff experience)	9 months / $1,100k	●	●●●	Enablement tech, procurement, finance	N/A	Lower impact / confidence	Revisit next cycle
Retail reshaping, close 5 underperforming stores and open 2 in high growth areas ($2m pa saving from year 2)	12 months / $4,000k	●●●	●●●●	Channels, people & culture, procurement	N/A	Lower impact / confidence	Revisit next cycle
Move to a 4-day work week, incl. training, tools, op model change to lift engagement and reduce churn (cost neutral)	12 months / $2,500k	●●	●●●●●	People & culture, all BUs	Significant workload on people leaders	Lower impact / confidence	Revisit next cycle

I have not yet seen a capital budgeting process that left everyone satisfied. The point is not to make stakeholders happy, but to allocate scarce resources in a way that achieves the best outcome for the business balancing both short- and long-term objectives. So once debates are done and the portfolio has settled, commit to it and get on with delivering it.

Making It Work

The Sudoku Method gives you a good structure, but there are also a few practical disciplines that will help run it effectively.

Decide or defer — but be explicit. Not all decisions need to be made at the same time, and in a complex decision web, investing effort and forcing premature calls on Tier 3 and 4 choices can be wasteful. If deferring a decision by a few weeks won't block any workstream, defer it as you'll have better information later. If it's holding up three teams, then decide now, even if the information is imperfect. The worst outcome isn't making an early call that needs revising. It's leaving a decision in limbo where nobody knows whether it's been made, deferred, or forgotten. Every decision on your map should have one of three labels: decided, deferred with a trigger to revisit, or in progress. No orphans.

Use "high-conviction hypotheses" to short-circuit. In complex projects, some upstream calls need to be made before you have full confidence in them — let's call them "high-conviction hypotheses" for now. But these hypotheses must not become corporate-speak for "we're not really committing". A high-conviction hypothesis is a decision with an explicit expiry condition: "We are proceeding on the basis that X is true. If Y emerges during Tier 3 analysis, we will revisit." It has the same rigour and governance as a committed decision. The only difference is that the team has pre-agreed the trigger for reopening it. Without that discipline, every Tier 1 and Tier 2 call risks becoming permanently provisional.

Complexity reinforces the fundamentals. It may be tempting to treat projects with infinite degrees of freedom as requiring a fundamentally different approach to decision-making. Luckily, they don't. The principles from the earlier chapters — right people, right culture, right framing, right process — apply just as much here. If anything, they matter more. The discipline, consistency and rigour become non-negotiables. In a simple decision environment, a mediocre team with unclear objectives might still land on a decent answer through sheer effort. In a decision web, the same team with the same lack of clarity will produce chaos. The 1% is harder to see, the circular dependencies amplify every misstep, and the consequences ripple further and faster.

The Sudoku Method gives you a way to navigate the most complex decision environments without drowning in them. But even with the right method, things go wrong. Complexity amplifies the number of variables and, as a result, the chances of failure. Drift, wrong questions, fake options, analysis paralysis, commitment failure, and refusal to pivot are all more likely and more damaging when decisions are interdependent. The next chapter explores these common pitfalls and why they keep emerging even in capable organisations.

Part Three

The Practice

Chapter 11:
Why Good Organisations Make Bad Decisions

"You don't rise to the level of your goals. You fall to the level of your systems."

— JAMES CLEAR

Organisations don't fail at decision-making because they lack smart people or good intentions. They fail because multiple forces — structural, cultural, and psychological — conspire to push even capable teams toward the path of least resistance. These forces operate quietly, consistently, and often with the unconscious cooperation of the people they are undermining.

By this point in the book, none of what follows should feel unfamiliar. You've already encountered these failure patterns between the lines of earlier chapters and case studies. What's worth doing now is putting them all on display in one place. Let's name them, understand where they come from, and see how they reinforce each other. This will help us demystify and diagnose the challenge.

This chapter is the diagnosis. We'll start with six recurring failure patterns that account for the vast majority of decision-making breakdowns, then unpack the forces that sustain them: operating model design, leadership and culture, cognitive biases, and individual mindsets. The next chapter is the treatment plan — what to do about all of it.

The Six Mortal Sins of Decision-Making

In my experience, the vast majority of decision-making failures can be traced back to six recurring patterns. I call them the six mortal sins.

Drift instead of decision: Perhaps the most common failure is not deciding at all. Teams and their leaders avoid asking hard questions or facing into uncomfortable choices, allowing direction to "emerge" through inertia, default settings, or incremental compromises. Work continues, meetings are held, slides are produced, but no one can point to a clear decision that explains why the team or organisation is doing what it's doing. Drift feels safe in the moment, but it is one of the most dangerous and expensive behaviours for an organisation.

Asking the wrong questions: When teams do engage in conscious decision-making, they often ask the wrong questions and solve the wrong problems. Instead of tackling the choices that move the needle, they gravitate toward choices they feel comfortable solving or where they can demonstrate some progress. Unfortunately, this approach is bound to create a lot of activity without much impact. The real danger is that despite the optics of progress, the core issue remains untouched. And typically, the longer it remains untouched, the harder it will be to solve.

Considering the wrong options: Even when the right question is on the table, the options considered can derail the outcome. In the previous chapters, we looked at the two common ways this manifests itself in organisations. Some teams consciously or unconsciously converge on a preferred answer and then justify it without genuinely exploring alternatives. They are effectively shoe-horning a recommendation. Others engage in a box-ticking exercise by manufacturing trivial or artificial choices solely to meet governance expectations. They are creating the illusion of rigour without substance.

Analysis paralysis: Some questions are fundamentally judgment-based. They require taking into account organisational values, beliefs, objectives, and guiding principles, not more data. Yet many organisations respond to uncertainty by commissioning more analysis, more modelling, and more scenario evaluations. Analysis paralysis is a symptom of discomfort with making a call in an ambiguous environment. Decisions stall when mathematical precision is used as an excuse to delay philosophical judgment or choice that is based on an imperfect set of information.

Recommendation or commitment failure: In many organisations, debate happens, but decisions don't land. Meetings end with "general alignment", "directional agreement", or a vague sense of progress. Either no explicit recommendation is made, or a recommendation is made with no one explicitly objecting or committing to it. Accountability remains diffuse, and decisions reopen weeks later. This pattern is particularly corrosive because it looks collaborative on the surface while eroding trust and momentum.

Failure to pivot when circumstances change: Finally, some decisions fail not because they were wrong at the time, but because organisations refuse to revisit them when new evidence emerges. Sunk costs, reputational concerns, and emotional attachment make it easier to stay the course than to acknowledge that the answer has changed. The result is persistence without justification — often framed as "sticking to the strategy", but in reality reflecting an inability to adapt and course-correct.

These six patterns can manifest independently or surface in combinations, reinforcing each other. Drift results in last-minute problems, which create urgency. Urgency results in rushed framing and wrong questions. Wrong questions bring up bad options. Bad options in an ambiguous environment can lead to analysis paralysis. Lack of confidence in the analysis prevents commitment. Lack of commitment fuels inertia, which in turn makes pivoting harder.

These sins arise when people choose the easier path in the moment. Avoiding the difficult question feels safer than asking it. Deferring a commitment feels more comfortable than making one. Sticking with a failing plan feels less painful than admitting it's broken. But as we'll see, the easy choice today almost always compounds into the hard life later.

If the mortal sins describe what goes wrong, the rest of this chapter unpacks why. In my experience, the root causes sit in four places:
- the operating model that governs how decisions are structured and resourced;
- the culture and leadership signals that shape how people actually behave within that model;

— the cognitive biases hardwired into human psychology that distort judgment under pressure; and

— the individual mindset traps that can make even the most talented leaders their own worst enemy.

Like the failure patterns, these four forces are interconnected. A fragmented operating model creates ambiguity, which leadership either resolves through clear signals or compounds through inconsistency. Biases flourish unless leaders and operating model proactively seek to counter those. And when egos enter the picture, it can override all three, turning a manageable structural problem into a chronic organisational dysfunction. Let's look at each of those.

Operating Model Failures

A common source of decision-making failure sits in the operating model itself. Many organisations invest heavily in strategy, frameworks, and talent, yet unintentionally design systems where good decisions are structurally hard to make and even harder to sustain.

Fragmented ownership that creates drift

A pattern that is all too common in large organisations looks like this: one group frames the problem, another evaluates options, a third approves the recommendation, a fourth executes it, and a fifth evaluates and monitors performance. Each group can be highly competent and act in good faith, yet no one truly owns the decision end-to-end.

When accountability is fragmented, decisions lose momentum. Teams only feel responsible for "their part" of the process, but not for the outcome. Emerging issues become "someone else's fault" and fixing those is definitely "someone else's responsibility". Hard trade-offs are deferred because they sit at the seams between teams' accountabilities. Questions that cut across silos are labelled "too hard" or "out of scope". Over time, if the organisation is lucky, direction may still emerge, but it's usually through the accumulation of small, tactical choices rather than deliberate intent. And more often than not the direction is far from optimal.

The drift becomes normalised and institutionalised. When the system doesn't clearly assign responsibility, people rarely go out of their way to take it. Unless, of course, you've stacked your teams with "make magic happen" individuals. But even the most talented people will struggle to get important stuff done despite the system and will eventually give up or leave.

Spaghetti vs Sushi Operating Model

A major financial services firm had an operating model that nobody designed. It just happened. Over many years, as senior leaders came and went, capabilities were pulled into different pockets of the business and left to drift. Each business unit ended up with its own strategy team, performance management function, operations and analytics capability. Central shared functions duplicated the same jobs. In some cases, teams across different units were competing for the same piece of work.

But the most crippling consequence was not the cost of duplication. It was the paralysis around decision-making. When a question arose, nobody could tell you who was responsible for the answer. Was it the business unit strategy team? The divisional strategy team? The enterprise strategy team? All three had a view, none had clear authority. Two-thirds of their effort was spent figuring out who was responsible rather than solving the problem.

When consultants were brought in, they struggled to even map the model and compared it to a tangled ball of spaghetti. Their proposed alternative was radically simple, like a piece of sushi: built around the teams closest to the customer. Strip out the layers, consolidate duplicated capabilities, give clear ownership to the people who serve the market.

The logic was hard to argue with, but executives who had spent years building their fiefdoms were unwilling to let go. The old model endured. The company continued to lose market share to competitors who could make decisions in days that took this organisation months.

Misaligned decision rights and execution responsibility

Another frequent failure occurs when decision authority sits far away from the consequences of execution. In some organisations, senior forums retain control over detailed choices despite being removed from day-to-day reality. Or similarly, teams are told that they are empowered, but critical decisions require multiple layers of endorsement.

When people are expected to execute decisions that they didn't shape or where their recommendations get frequently overruled, they learn to protect themselves. Recommendations become vague, timelines and budgets get sandbagged, analysis expands — sometimes to defer the unpopular choice that is forced upon the team. Re-litigation can also become common because decisions are never truly owned in the first place.

The irony is that this often happens in the name of risk management. In practice, it increases risk by slowing pace of decision-making and diffusing accountability.

Governance that optimises for optics

Governance forums are meant to create discipline, but too often, they do the opposite. In many organisations, governance becomes a stage-managed exercise whereby decisions are presented as "done deals". If the real debate happens, it happens offline. Formal forums exist purely as decoration, rather than to raise tensions and offer space for constructive challenge. As a result, shoe-horning flourishes, where a preferred solution quietly consolidates support long before alternatives are meaningfully explored.

One of the manifestations of it that we've discussed in the "What" chapter is when governance processes force teams into artificial choice-making by presenting multiple options that no one believes in simply to tick a box. This satisfies process requirements but adds little value for the organisation.

Another common issue is applying "one-way-door" governance to "two-way-door" decisions. Subjecting low-consequence, reversible choices to the rigorous approval processes, multi-stage committee reviews, and sign-off chains is an example of "overgovernance tax". Part of the problem for many organisations is having those forums and committees as permanent fixtures. If the committee exists, it will inevitably be looking for stuff to govern — and in most cases it will succeed.

The $300,000 Cup of Coffee

A business unit of a bank needed to add a new search category to their app (alongside the existing dozen categories). It felt like a straightforward configuration task that should have been a Tier 4 decision with a sprint-long execution at most. Instead, as the company was running a strict governance model with "one front door", this feature had to enter the formal estimation process.

The requirement was presented to a forum of twenty-five participants spanning digital, technology, architecture, data, delivery, marketing, and channels to name a few. Each team, facing uncertainty and keen to hedge their commitments, submitted conservative estimates. When consolidated, this small feature ballooned to three hundred thousand dollars and three months of work.

Nobody questioned whether the process was proportionate to the problem. The governance machinery simply did what it was designed to do — comprehensively, thoroughly, and entirely unnecessarily.

Frustrated by the estimate, the initiative lead approached the developer who actually owned the functionality. His response, over a coffee, was immediate: provide a structured data file from another team and he could turn it on straight away. By week's end, the feature was live — at the cost of a cup of coffee.

The scarier part? If the organisation actually had three hundred thousand dollars to spend, they would most likely have spent it and taken the full three months — a textbook case of Parkinson's Law, where work expands to fill the time and budget allocated. The overgovernance tax here wasn't just theoretical. It nearly turned a one-hour task into a quarter-long project.

Not only does inappropriate governance create the false appearance of rigour without the substance, it wastes valuable organisational resources.

If the choice is made "offline" through a "captain's call", it's better to be straight about it, rather than getting the teams to spin up props and put up a performance to make it look like a real thing.

Overloaded pipelines and competing priorities

Operating model failure also shows up in how work is sequenced and workload is managed. When organisations lack discipline in starting and stopping work, decision quality degrades rapidly. Teams are asked to progress multiple initiatives in parallel, each framed as urgent and important. As context switching increases cognitive load, attention starts to fragment, which inevitably impacts quality and performance. The teams start gravitating towards finishing at least something, whatever is easiest, to feel progress, rather than finishing what's most important.

In this environment, asking and answering the wrong questions can feel productive because it creates a feeling of momentum. Analysis paralysis can become a go-to tool of workload management because it can delay further commitments. Using non-value adding busy work as a deferral or optics management mechanism is obviously wasteful from an organisational perspective.

Focus, as discussed earlier in the book, is not a mindset problem alone. It is a real operating constraint. If not adequately managed, it can severely impact the quality and pace of decision-making in the overloaded teams.

The wrong incentives

Incentives, whether related to specific target metrics or to adherence to cultural norms, compound the problem.

A common and very tangible manifestation of misaligned incentives is when multiple teams involved in a decision have a different sets of objectives and key results. One team may be focused on sales volume, another one on margin. This makes it difficult to find a mutually acceptable choice. A lot of time and energy gets wasted in debates that are inherently unresolvable, unless, of course, higher order objectives get realigned between the teams.

Another manifestation is when organisations unintentionally reward consistency over getting to the right answer, going through the motions over delivering outcomes, and sticking to the plan over learning. Teams can learn that it's safer to defend a flawed decision than to reopen it, or safer to go with the choice that senior executives prefer rather than raise "career limiting" concerns.

People quickly figure out what's praised and what you get a slap on the wrist for. Those experiences of "carrots and sticks" accumulate, creating internal narratives that can be very different from what's on the organisational values posters. When the watercooler narratives diverge from the townhall presentations, disengagement and even resentment set in.

Misalignment of incentives is one of the most potent impediments to good decision-making that needs to be addressed head-on.

When decision rights, execution responsibility and incentives are misaligned, disciplined decision-making becomes almost impossible. In the next section, we'll turn from structure to behaviour — examining how leadership signals and mindset issues subtly reinforce these same failure patterns, even in organisations with otherwise sound operating models.

Culture and Leadership: the Signals That Shape Behaviour

Even with a well-designed operating model, decision-making quality comes down to how people behave — and behaviour in organisations is shaped far less by what's written in the values statement than by what gets rewarded, tolerated, and punished in practice. That's why culture and leadership belong in the same section: organisational culture is not something that exists independently of leaders. It is the accumulated output of thousands of leadership signals, large and small, deliberate and accidental, compounding over time until they harden into "the way things work around here".

We touched on the role of leadership in Chapter 1 and explored cultural aspects like focus, openness, clarity and speed in Chapter 7. What we need to address here are the specific cultural patterns and leadership behaviours that directly feed the six mortal sins — often in organisations that, on paper, have all the right frameworks in place.

Risk and ambiguity aversion

Many organisations develop a deep institutional discomfort with making decisions under uncertainty. Teams feel they need overwhelming evidence before committing to a course of action, and leaders reinforce this by asking "Are we sure?" far more often than "What's the cost of waiting for better evidence?"

The result is a culture where analysis becomes a safety blanket. Business cases get recycled through multiple rounds of refinement because no one feels safe enough to make the call. Every recommendation comes hedged with caveats. Timelines stretch as teams chase an ever-shifting threshold of confidence that never arrives, because most consequential decisions are inherently ambiguous — that's what makes them consequential.

This is a direct feeder of analysis paralysis and drift. And it often starts at the top. When leaders consistently demand certainty before acting, or punish calls that don't work out regardless of the quality of reasoning behind them, they train the organisation to avoid committing to anything that might be wrong. Over time, the safest career move becomes "wait for more data" — which in practice means "wait for someone else to decide".

The Day That Cost Two Months

A digital team was building a new customer-facing feature that needed to go live ahead of a major marketing campaign. The vendor that managed the platform operated on a fortnightly release cycle: if you miss the window, come back in two weeks. The team had a design question that needed sign-off from the product owner. It was not a difficult call, but the product owner wanted to "double check" it with the senior executive who was travelling and asked the team to hold off until the following day.

That one day pushed the build past the vendor's release cut-off. The next available release slot fell on the UAT environment freeze due to core system upgrade, which meant testing had to be delayed. The revised testing timeline landed on the communications blackout period, so marketing had to push the launch further out.

What followed was two-month delay with cumbersome replanning involving two dozen people across digital, product, marketing, and the vendor, all to solve a problem caused by a twenty-four-hour delay on a decision that should have taken ten minutes. Nobody made a wrong call. Someone just didn't make it in time.

Consensus-seeking and conflict avoidance

Closely related is the cultural reflex toward niceness. In many organisations, particularly those that pride themselves on being collaborative, there is an unspoken expectation that decisions should feel comfortable for everyone involved. Dissent is treated not as a valuable input but as a social transgression — something to be smoothed over, reframed, or sidelined in the interest of maintaining harmony.

The cost of such "harmony" can be substantial, but hard to notice. Options that make people uncomfortable don't get surfaced. Concerns that might create tension don't get raised. Recommendations get sanded down to the lowest common denominator until they're so bland that no one would find anything to react to — and too weak to actually solve any problem. Meetings end with "alignment" that is just the absence of objection.

This is the engine behind wrong recommendation failure. And it's almost always a leadership problem dressed up as a team dynamic. When leaders reward alignment over challenge, visibly prefer harmony to honest debate, or react with irritation when assumptions get questioned, they create the conditions for consensus-seeking to flourish. It takes remarkably few instances of a leader responding badly to dissent for an entire team to learn not to rock the boat.

Focus on optics rather than real outcomes

When organisations prioritise how things look over what they actually achieve, decision-making turns into a stage performance. Governance forums exist to validate decisions already made rather than to genuinely challenge them. Business cases are crafted to survive scrutiny rather than to be correct. Progress reports emphasise activity and milestones rather than outcomes and learning.

The optics trap is self-reinforcing: once teams figure out that leaders care more about the narrative than the substance, they start investing their energy accordingly. Instead of putting effort into problem-solving and getting stuff done, people endlessly polish their slide decks, craft reports to make them more optimistic, wordsmith board papers into works of bureaucratic art. Meanwhile, the real issues accumulate underneath, and by the time they blow up in the face the cost and complexity of addressing them has gone out of control.

This directly fuels drift and the wrong-questions sin. When the measure of success is "Does this look good?" rather than "Does this solve the problem?" people gravitate toward what's visible and reportable rather than what's difficult and important.

Leaning into everything

One of the common leadership missteps is conflating authority with decision quality. As we discussed in Chapter 1, seniority does not automatically confer better judgment, especially when it comes to complex, multi-faceted problems. Yet many leaders feel compelled to weigh in on everything — a suggestion here, a "here's the right answer" there, a "have you considered" probe that the team didn't ask for and doesn't need.

When a leader leans in on mission-critical choices, teams will understand and value it. But when the leaning in bit is indiscriminate, it crosses the red micromanagement line and produces a predictable response: teams stop thinking independently and showing initiative. Instead, they wait for the leader to give them a nudge and provide value-adding guidance on how to proceed. What's the point of being proactive, developing options and doing analysis if the leader is going to come in and show us the way?

When "Exploration" Means "Just Do It"

A large organisation had invested heavily in repositioning itself as a place where teams shaped their own backlog and had genuine ownership of customer experience. On paper, it was a modern, highly autonomous operating model.

In practice, leadership hadn't caught up. Senior executives would periodically discover a new technology or solution and hand it to teams for "exploration". The teams would have welcomed genuine exploration — an honest assessment of whether the idea solved a real customer problem. But it became clear that these suggestions arrived with an unspoken expectation to prioritise and make it work.

The teams tried to objectively evaluate the handed-down ideas, challenging assumptions, comparing alternatives, or recommending against. However, the feedback they got was far from positive. They were seen as closed-minded, not thinking like enterprise players, not considering the long-term potential. After a few rounds of "constructive challenge", the teams adapted. They stopped asking "what's the right solution to the problem?" and started asking "what's the most effective use of the solution or piece of technology that we've been given?"

After a string of unsuccessful launches, months of misdirected effort, and millions in wasted investment the leadership recognised that the empowerment model they had publicly championed was, in practice, a good old top-down directive culture with some misleading marketing spin on it.

Being the bottleneck

Closely related is the gatekeeping pattern. Leaders who struggle to let go inject themselves into decisions at all levels, often with limited knowledge and without appreciating the drag they create. When decisions routinely escalate to the same few individuals, throughput collapses and decision quality deteriorates. Those leaders can be highly competent, but because they are trying to be the clearing house for too many calls creating a "convince me" burden for the teams who have the deep understanding and have done the thinking. When the teams see that the decisions they are perfectly equipped to make need to get escalated and those escalations take a lot of time and effort, they get disempowered and disengage.

Another angle to it is that leaders who hold on to too many decisions inevitably find themselves overwhelmed and overworked. Important choices slip off the radar or get delayed unnecessarily, creating a material friction within the organisation — costing money and, more importantly, time. The most damaging long-term outcome is learned helplessness. Even the best teams stop owning problems and start waiting for the boss.

When a Leader Becomes the Bottleneck

Following a major transformation, a business unit welcomed a new senior leader. The team they inherited was high performing and accustomed to making decisions quickly and autonomously — within clear guardrails.

As part of their ongoing work, the team identified an opportunity to accelerate a long-delayed project. The scope was modest, and while it hadn't been explicitly budgeted for, the team believed, based on prior experience, that the cost could be absorbed without material impact on their financials.

The team flagged the opportunity to the new leader early. Acknowledging they were still getting across the business, the leader asked for time. Weeks passed. Follow-ups were polite but increasingly pointed. No explicit concern was raised, but no decision was made either.

As the delay dragged on, frustration grew. Team confidence started to waver, not because the decision was complex, but because the absence of a clear direction made it impossible to plan or commit.

Two months later, the issue was raised directly: should the team proceed, or should the project be killed? The response was quick and confident: "Of course you can proceed."

It was a relief, but the team was still confused. From their perspective, nothing substantive had changed. There were no new risks, no additional information, and no meaningful trade-offs uncovered during the delay. What had changed was momentum. A small decision that could have taken days had consumed two months.

In this case, the leader didn't intend to slow the organisation down, but by not making a call promptly, they did exactly that.

For high-performing teams, prolonged uncertainty can signal mistrust and erode autonomy.

The irony is that leaders who become bottlenecks often do so with good intent — reduce risk, to unblock progress, ensure strategic alignment, or bring extra clarity. In practice, the pattern erodes ownership and trains dependency. The organisation learns to wait for the boss rather than to own the problem and solve it effectively.

Inconsistency: saying one thing, doing another

Perhaps the most damaging signal that leaders can send is inconsistency between their words and their actions. It shows up when leaders say they want debate but react defensively when challenged. It shows up when they encourage autonomy but intervene at the first sign of uncertainty. It shows up when they publicly commit to a decision and then relitigate it behind closed doors.

Each instance of inconsistency teaches teams that what the leader says and what the leader does are different things. Over time, people stop listening to the stated values and start reading the actual behaviour. They either begin mirroring the inconsistency themselves or default to what feels safest — and what feels safest is almost never what produces the best decision.

The most destructive aspect of inconsistency isn't a bad outcome for a specific project, but systemic degradation of the corporate culture. When teams don't trust that the stated rules and narratives are real, some stop listening and playing by the rules, others start hedging everything — recommendations, timelines, commitments. The organisation fills up with ambiguity that didn't need to exist, and every decision takes longer.

Ultimately, structures and operating models can enable good decisions, but leaders through their daily actions and inactions determine whether those structures are used as intended — or quietly bypassed. Decision-making culture is shaped far less by what leaders say than by what they do, and what they tolerate — particularly under pressure. Even with a clean operating model and well-aligned incentives, disciplined decision-making will not take root if leadership behaviour works against it. This is where many organisations struggle.

Biases and Cognitive Shortcuts to Watch Out for

Over millennia, the human brain has evolved into a remarkably efficient decision-making machine — and that's precisely the problem. Under pressure, it defaults to shortcuts that prioritise speed over accuracy, comfort over truth, and pattern-matching over fresh thinking. Rolf Dobelli catalogued ninety-nine of these cognitive biases in The Art of Thinking Clearly. You don't need to memorise all of them, but a handful are so prevalent in organisational decision-making that they deserve a spot on your radar.

Confirmation bias is the tendency to seek out evidence that supports what you already believe and ignore what contradicts it. In practice, this means teams unconsciously build the case for the answer they've already landed on. Options evaluations become advocacy documents. Contradictory data gets omitted or at best footnoted rather than confronted head on. This is the driving force behind shoe-horning — the third mortal sin.

Anchoring is the brain's habit of latching onto the first number or idea it encounters and using it as a reference point for everything that follows. In a business case review, whichever option is presented first tends to frame the discussion. In a negotiation, the opening number sets the range. Teams rarely notice it happening, which makes it particularly dangerous. Anchoring is a potent bias that can sway complex decisions away from the optimal choice.

Sunk cost bias keeps organisations investing in decisions that are well past their expiry date. The behaviour is emotional, not rational: "We've come this far, we can't stop now." The more time, money, and reputation that's been poured into a course of action, the harder it becomes to walk away — even when every piece of evidence says you should. This is the primary fuel behind the sixth mortal sin: failure to pivot.

Value-Destroying Sunk Cost Bias

In the competitive landscape of metal 3D printing, a small engineering startup developed a groundbreaking printer capable of using diverse metals such as aluminium, copper, titanium, and stainless steel, to name a few. The technology turned out to be cutting-edge in speed and precision. It attracted a lot of interest at the international exhibitions.

Eager to accelerate technological advancement and growth, the startup approached a major state-owned conglomerate with a partnership proposal to use their technology and scale fast. These tech geniuses weren't after making money; they wanted to drive metal 3D printing adoption as a way to increase manufacturing efficiency across many sectors.

The leader of the conglomerate division was impressed. He admitted that the start-up was two years ahead of them in terms of technological maturity.

However, the conglomerate has invested tens of millions of dollars in its own 3D printing technology over the previous five years. It also had a dedicated business unit with substantial resources committed to advancing their own admittedly inferior solution.

Despite the startup's more advanced technology, the fear of internal reputational impact, unwillingness to face into potential operating model changes, and the sunk costs already incurred led to a decision to continue with in-house development rather than to partner. Commercial aspects have not even been a consideration.

The opportunity for the conglomerate was obvious — leapfrog two years of research and development to get ahead of the market. The cost of access to technology would have been a tiny fraction of the annual run cost of their in-house R&D team.

Loss aversion is closely related to sunk cost bias. It is the tendency to perceive losses roughly twice as intensely as equivalent gains. This makes pivoting feel disproportionately painful and staying the course feel deceptively safe. It also explains why organisations are far more willing to invest in protecting what they have than in pursuing something better. It can also manifest in the capital budgeting decisions that we looked at in the previous chapter. Loss aversion skews allocation towards the short-term higher-certainty initiatives away from long-term opportunities and enablers that will unlock value in the future.

Overconfidence bias leads leaders and teams to overestimate their knowledge, underestimate risks, and commit to plans with insufficient margin for error. It's the reason so many business cases assume everything will go right and so few include a credible downside scenario. Overconfidence doesn't just affect individuals, it compounds in groups, where mutual reinforcement creates a shared illusion of certainty. If the corporate culture does not encourage constructive challenge, overconfidence can lead to organisations falling for their own fairy tales like we'll see in the WeWork case study in the next chapter.

Groupthink is the tendency for teams to prioritise harmony and consensus over honest evaluation. When the social cost of dissent is high, or at least perceived to be high, people self-censor. The result is decisions that everyone privately doubts but nobody publicly challenges. Groupthink is particularly dangerous because it produces the appearance of alignment, making flawed decisions look robust until reality intervenes.

These six are far from the only traps. Dobelli's catalogue includes dozens more that shape organisational decisions. Survivorship bias causes us to study successes and ignore the far larger pool of failures, drawing conclusions from an incomplete picture — "Company X did this and thrived" without asking how many companies did the same thing and didn't. The halo effect leads us to assume that a person or organisation that excels in one area must be competent in others, which is how a charismatic leader's enthusiasm for an idea can bypass the scrutiny that idea deserves. Authority bias leads us to defer to the opinion of someone with status or credentials, which is the cognitive cousin of the HIPPO problem we discussed in Chapter 6. And the planning fallacy ensures that nearly every project timeline and budget is optimistic, because we consistently underestimate the time, cost, and complexity of tasks we haven't yet started even when our track record of previous estimates tells us otherwise.

These biases don't disappear with intelligence or experience. Quite the opposite, senior and highly educated teams can be even more vulnerable, because they are better than an average punter at rationalising their preferences and more accustomed to being right. Awareness also does little to cure those. What we need is to build processes and leadership habits that actively counteract these shortcuts. We'll return to that in the next chapter.

One more thing on biases. Every bias discussed above can be amplified in a world where AI is doing more of the heavy lifting. Models trained on historical data will faithfully reproduce the blind spots of past decisions on which they were trained. If your organisation has a pattern of confirmation bias in how it selects evidence, an AI tool trained on that same evidence base will confirm it faster and more convincingly. When was the last time ChatGPT disagreed with you? If anchoring has been distorting your forecasts, the AI will anchor on the same distorted data. You get the point. The disciplines in this book (openness, radical transparency, constructive challenge) become even more essential as a counterweight to the biases that may be exacerbated by AI tools.

The Three Mindset Viruses

Ego is the common thread running through the failure patterns we've mapped in this chapter. It's the force that makes leaders cling to flawed decisions, dismiss dissent, hoard authority, and avoid accountability. But ego doesn't always present itself in obvious ways. Three specific manifestations are worth calling out, because each has the potential to make organisational life miserable — and two or three combined can be lethal. Worse, all three are infectious: they spread through teams, normalise quickly, and are extraordinarily difficult to "cure" once embedded.

Hubris is the belief that you know the answer and your answer is way better than everyone else's. It manifests as impatience with analysis, dismissal of dissenting views, and a pattern of decisions made on instinct and then defended long past the point of reason.

Hubris can fuel several of the mortal sins at once. It bypasses proper framing — why ask questions when you already know. It narrows options — why explore alternatives to the obvious answer. And also blocks pivoting — why change course when you have been right all along. The antidote to hubris virus is humility. Not the self-deprecating kind, but the genuine intellectual humility of someone who knows that the world is complex and their perspective of it is never perfect or complete.

Entitlement is the belief that the rules shouldn't apply to you the same way and you "deserve better". It shows up as leaders who expect special treatment, bypass governance that everyone else follows, and assign responsibility for failures while retaining credit for success.

In decision-making, entitled leaders poison the well because their teams learn that the rules apply selectively and that the decisions go wherever the entitled leader wants. The antidote to entitlement virus is responsibility. The proactive ownership kind that we explored in Chapter 6 talking about the "Who". A "make magic happen" leader genuinely believes that leadership is more of a service responsibility than a status marker.

Victimhood is the belief that external forces (euphemism for "other people") are to blame. It manifests as a chronic inability to own outcomes. "The market turned", "we weren't given enough resources", "the other team dropped the ball". Victimhood is corrosive because it undermines agency for the self-proclaimed "victim". It is also infectious for the people around them. It breeds "us vs them" mentality. If everything is someone else's fault, there's nothing to learn and nothing to fix.

This mindset can set teams and even entire organisations on a downward spiral. Rather than confronting hard choices, people get accustomed to blaming circumstances, market conditions or "the system" for the lack of progress. The antidote to victimhood virus is gratitude. A genuine appreciation of things that go ok with an orientation towards what you can control and make better, rather than what you can't.

When any of the three viruses show up in individuals or teams, they will degrade decision quality and pace. But the real danger is when they combine. No framework, no governance, no amount of talented people around them will compensate for a SME or a leader who is simultaneously hubristic (won't listen), entitled (won't follow the rules), and self-victimised (won't own outcomes). If you recognise any of these patterns in yourself or in others, address them before they metastasise.

The forces we have discussed in this chapter — structural misalignment, cultural and leadership behaviours, cognitive wiring, and the quiet corrosion of ego — are why capable organisations keep making the same decision-making mistakes. They are the predictable consequences of how organisations are designed and led. The important thing to remember is that none of them are inevitable. In the next chapter, we'll turn from diagnosis to action: the leadership disciplines, organisational practices, and measurement that break these patterns — and keep them from returning.

Chapter 12:
Leading Organisations from Good to Great

"Hard choices, easy life. Easy choices, hard life."

— JERZY GREGOREK

If the previous chapter was a diagnosis, this one is the treatment plan, or at the very least a set of essential components for one. Understanding why organisations make bad decisions is necessary, but not sufficient. Knowing the problem doesn't, by itself, change anything. Now let's get into the question of what to do about it.

The answer comes in three parts. The first is around the leadership standards that determine whether leaders, in the broadest sense of that word, reinforce the failure patterns or drive the organisation to success. The second is around organisational practices that make good decision-making the default rather than the exception, regardless of who happens to be in the room. The third is around ensuring that the organisation is genuinely rather than superficially aligned on the goals and objectives.

We'll start with the leader.

Leadership Standards

In the previous chapter, we explored how leadership behaviour entrenches the very failure patterns organisations are trying to escape. Now we need to talk about the personal standards that leaders must hold themselves to if they want decision-making discipline to flourish around them.

Every organisation needs to define the leadership standards that are aligned with their values and aspirations. However, there are six outlined below that would work well in most environments. It's important to note that these are not abstract textbook principles that get slapped on the intranet site and talked about at corporate townhalls. All of the standards should be practical and readily observable behaviours that teams notice, internalise, and eventually replicate.

"It's my fault"

We covered extreme ownership in Chapter 6: the leader who says "go" owns the outcome, full stop. The leadership standard is to practise it visibly. How often have you seen a leader standing up in front of their team admitting that they made a wrong call? And that's the problem.

When a leader draws attention to their own misjudgement — "I got this wrong, here's what I've learned, and here's what we're doing about it" — it makes it safe for others to acknowledge mistakes early. Once the senior leader takes full accountability, team members will almost always step up to share the burden. It never happens the other way. Blame that gets "delegated down" destroys trust faster than almost anything else.

No amount of polished corporate brochureware and inspirational keynote speakers can deliver the credibility that a leader builds by publicly owning a failure.

Turning a Terrible Idea into a Useful Experiment

A senior leader, during an informal conversation with a partner who operated in an adjacent category, learned that direct mail campaigns had been delivering extraordinary results for them. It was counterintuitive. Who reads snail mail these days? But the logic was surprisingly compelling: anti-spam regulations and rising postage costs had dramatically reduced the volume of promotional mail being sent, leaving letterboxes almost empty. When customers did receive something physical, they actually opened and read it, whereas a few years earlier most of it would go straight into the bin.

The leader brought the insight back to the team, who were sceptical. Their category had longer purchase cycles, so the rapid sales uplift the partner had seen didn't feel replicable. Running a physical mail campaign was also a forgotten art that required significant effort: developing creative, arranging customer data extracts, lining up a print house, coordinating distribution. A lot of effort for an unclear outcome didn't feel like the right thing to do, given numerous other initiatives underway.

The leader pushed ahead anyway, redirecting some media budget from proven digital channels to fund a small-scale campaign with around 30,000 promotional letters. The team put their best foot forward: the creative looked sharp, the call to action was clear, and the analytics tools were configured to closely monitor the sales funnel.

On the day the letters hit mailboxes, nothing happened. Web traffic showed no meaningful incremental activity. Phone queues didn't budge. Within a week, just six sales could be attributed to the campaign. At several thousand dollars in acquisition cost per sale, it was not a success by any measure.

Before anyone had the chance to say "told you so", the leader gathered the team and took full ownership. It was a terrible idea, but a valuable lesson. They now knew, with hard evidence rather than gut feel, that direct mail didn't work for their business and they wouldn't be doing it again. No hedging, no attempt to reframe, no suggestion that maybe with a different target audience or creative it might have worked. Just a clean acknowledgement: I pushed for this, it didn't deliver, I learned my lesson, let's move on.

One team member later reflected that after that conversation it no longer felt like a collective failure. It felt like a useful experiment that ended with an actionable insight, although not the one everyone had hoped for.

When the leader owns the miss, the team stops spending energy on self-protection and starts spending it on the next important decision.

Managing reality rather than optics

If you find yourself asking "How will this look?" before "Is this right for the business and our customers?" you've crossed into optics territory. The trap manifests in ways so normalised they barely register: the appearance of progress rather than hard yards, vanity metrics that are easy to hit rather than hard metrics that matter, performative alignment rather than genuine debate.

The standard is boringly simple — prioritise substance over spin, consistently. And call out spin constructively when you come across it. This doesn't mean ignoring stakeholder management or public perception, but rather refusing to let optics override an honest assessment of what's right and wrong, and what's working vs what looks good on paper. Leaders must not kid themselves — their teams can see through the smoke and mirrors, and trust will be the first victim. When a leader honestly calls a spade a spade even when it hurts, trust is reinforced.

47-Billion-Dollar Illusion

WeWork spent years selling a narrative that bore little resemblance to its economics. Valued at $47 billion at its peak, the company positioned itself as a technology platform "elevating the world's consciousness". The reality was a commercial lease arbitrage that lost money on virtually every location. Losses grew year after year while the leadership team kept projecting profitability was just around the corner.

The board gave the founder long-term voting control, allowed him to personally invest in buildings leased back to WeWork, and looked the other way as governance norms were quietly abandoned. When the IPO prospectus forced the financials into public view, the gap between the story and the spreadsheet was too wide to bridge. The valuation collapsed by over 80% in weeks. The company eventually filed for bankruptcy in 2023, destroying tens of billions in investor value.

It's important to recognise that the leadership failure wasn't a single bad decision. It was a sustained unwillingness to face reality when reality was uncomfortable. The meetings that ended with the narrative unchallenged, and the board sessions that prioritised optics over economics, were decisions too. They just weren't recognised as such until it was too late.

"When I find new information, I change my mind"

The quote is attributed to John Maynard Keynes, and the punchline is the follow-up: "What do you do, sir?"

A good leader takes a position. A great leader revises that position when circumstances change, and does so openly. This is not back-flipping — it's judgment in action, and it's rare because we've collectively decided that consistency is a virtue even when the facts have moved. It's hard, given that most of what we see in the media treats changing your mind almost as a taboo: politicians never back off even on the most obvious mistakes, to avoid looking weak or flippant.

The discipline is twofold. First, consciously challenge your own positions by looking for flaws, not just supporting evidence. Second, when you do change your mind, say so explicitly and thank the people who helped you get there. "I've changed my mind based on what I've heard" is one of the most powerful things a leader can say because it gives everyone else permission to think clearly rather than politically.

The power of "no"

The Focus discipline from chapter 7 applies to organisations. This standard is its personal twin. The same discipline, but now applied to your own calendar, your own commitments, and your own instinct to say yes.

When in doubt, treat "no" as the default until conviction dictates otherwise. Don't sit on the fence. Say a clear, honest "no, and here's why" rather than a tentative "let's park this" that everyone interprets as "ask me again next quarter". Every meeting you didn't need to attend, every initiative you sponsored out of politeness, every "quick favour" you said yes to — those are decisions too, and they all add up. Even if relatively small, those unnecessary "yeses" compound over time, driving complexity and workload for the leader and their teams. Done respectfully, "no" is clarifying and liberating, even when it's uncomfortable.

If in Doubt — It's Out

A large financial services organisation decided to merge two customer-facing apps into one, combining the best of both to simplify the experience and improve engagement.

The strategy was sound — many companies across sectors were starting to consolidate their digital assets. The problem was scale: migrating dozens of features from the satellite app into the main platform would take over two years and consume a substantial share of the enterprise's delivery capacity. The business didn't have two years. It needed to start showing results within twelve months.

The leadership team had to pivot from a "full migration" approach to a ruthlessly prioritised subset of the features that customers valued most, delivered in an order designed to generate outcomes early rather than comprehensiveness eventually.

The approach that they used was blunt and effective: "If in doubt — it's out". A feature needed to be an absolute must-have to earn its place on the migration list. Everything else was unapologetically parked until the legacy app was eventually decommissioned.

It was very uncomfortable: people that owned capabilities in the satellite app didn't love hearing that their feature wasn't making the cut. But the discipline held, and the result was a focused program that started delivering customer value within just six months rather than disappearing into a multi-year integration that would have tested everyone's patience and credibility.

You can only lean on that which resists

Chapter 7 made the case for why constructive challenge matters. Chapter 11 showed what happens when it's absent. The leadership standard is where it gets personal: are you actually doing it?

The practical test can be uncomfortable. Ask yourself: does your team challenge you regularly? I mean genuinely challenge — not ask polite questions and skirt around the issue. If the answer is no, you either have a team that thinks exactly like you, or you have not created an environment where disagreement feels safe. Either way, the quality of your decisions is suffering.

The discipline is threefold. First, openly challenge your own positions by looking for flaws, not just supporting evidence. Second, when your team challenges you, or each other, constructively, recognise it and encourage it. One of the most powerful things that a leader can do is make a big (positive) deal out of situations where the course of action was changed due to someone's constructive challenge. Third, back your team and colleagues who do it, even if the constructive challenge mindset has not been widely accepted in the broader organisation. It takes time, so build a trusted coalition.

Attack the Problem, Not the Person

When Andy Grove ran Intel in the 1980s and 1990s, he built a culture he called "constructive confrontation". The rules were explicit that anyone could challenge anyone, regardless of seniority, provided the challenge was aimed at the idea and not the person. A junior engineer with a better argument could, and was expected to, take on a vice president. Grove subjected himself to the same treatment. The culture was egalitarian in its enforcement, and that's what made it work.

The most consequential test came when Intel was losing money in its core memory chip business. It was a challenge from within, not a top-down epiphany, that helped Grove make the call to abandon memory chips entirely and bet the company on microprocessors. It became one of the most pivotal strategic decisions in technology history.

The cautionary footnote matters just as much as the success story. After Grove stepped back, the culture gradually lost its "constructive" half. Management ranks started putting themselves above the practice while still wielding it on people below them. The fierce debate survived, but the psychological safety and equal application didn't. As one former employee put it in 2007, constructive confrontation became "a licence for assholes to be assholes".

What had been a tool for better decisions turned into plain aggression dressed in cultural language. The principle only works when the leader who demands dissent also demonstrates, personally and visibly, how to receive it.

Great leaders get out of the way

There are two urges that leaders need to resist if they want their teams to become strong decision-makers. First, they must not hoard the decision-making authority, and let go of the vast majority of decisions, where their team is capable of solving those. Second, they must not try to "add value" or contribute to everything their team does.

As we've discussed in the diagnostic chapter above, some leaders feel compelled to control all the decisions. This does two kinds of damage that compound each other: these leaders clog the system, becoming a bottleneck, and, equally damaging, they signal distrust. If you've built the right team and set clear guardrails, most decisions should never reach your desk. You should only be finding out about them as an FYI. Your job is to decide which decisions truly require your involvement — the genuine 1%-ers — and to explicitly delegate the rest with a clear mandate: "This is yours. I trust you. Keep me informed".

Even when decisions are delegated down, some leaders succumb to the temptation to "add value". This constant leaning-in can be subtle and well-intentioned, which is what makes it annoying for the team and dangerous for the culture. Often the input is genuine and valuable, but the cumulative effect is corrosive: teams learn that the leader will always tinker, so they stop finishing their own thinking.

The standard is to distinguish between situations that genuinely need your input and situations where your best contribution is silence. One of the litmus tests could be "Is my contribution going to significantly change the outcome or save the team a lot of effort?" If not — keep it to yourself, however hard it is. If you find it hard to hold back your "contributions", write or type them first in the notepad, review and then decide whether to share. When capable teams are trusted with full autonomy, they often find solutions that leadership would never have thought of.

14 Months in 14 Weeks

A health insurer had identified a genuine gap in post-hospital care. Customers discharged after major operations, particularly elderly patients with post-operative wounds that take weeks to heal, were falling through the cracks between high-acuity hospital-in-the-home services and standard community care where they were largely left to manage on their own with occasional GP visits.

The opportunity was fairly obvious in terms of both health outcomes and patient experience. And yet it had been sitting in the "too hard basket" for a couple of years. Senior leadership didn't have the bandwidth to lean in and problem-solve, and the teams closer to the issue hadn't felt empowered to push it forward without executive sponsorship.

What had to change was the way of working, including how leadership engaged. The teams responsible for care delivery, patient experience, and clinical oversight came together and agreed on a plan. All that was required from their respective executives was to fully delegate decision-making and execution to their people and commit to fortnightly check-ins. Those check-ins were not forums for seeking executive endorsement. They served two purposes: creating full transparency on the progress, and helping to remove roadblocks and constraints. The executives' job was just to clear the path.

This was not a trivial undertaking. It required developing a new Model of Care, establishing funding arrangements, creating referral pathways with hospitals, building escalation protocols for patients whose recovery was at risk, engaging and briefing hundreds of nurses across the country, and setting up outcome monitoring and reporting. A project of this scope would normally have taken the organisation fourteen months. It was delivered in fourteen weeks. Just over three months from the day of the initial meeting at which the teams got the green light, the service launched nationally.

This initiative demonstrated a pace virtually unheard of in healthcare. And it was enabled by the executives simply getting out of the way and letting their capable teams make magic happen.

A big part of leaders' craft is in creating conditions where solutions like this emerge, without getting involved in every problem — and then having the wisdom to admire the result rather than tinker with it.

Building Capability in the Organisation

Leadership standards are necessary, but by themselves insufficient. Even the most disciplined leader operates inside a system, and if that system isn't designed to produce good decisions, individual effort will be overwhelmed by institutional gravity. This section is about the organisational infrastructure that makes good decision-making the default rather than something that depends on who happens to be in the room.

Design the decision architecture

Earlier in this book we identified the decisions that matter most and built a tiering framework to match effort to consequence. But knowing which decisions matter is different from knowing who gets to make them. The most common organisational failure isn't that the wrong decision gets made — it's that no one is sure whose decision it is in the first place, so it either gets made by default (whoever happens to be in the room) or not made at all (because everyone assumes someone else will do it).

The fix is explicit decision rights. Not a ten-page roles-and-responsibilities charter that lives in a shared folder no one opens, but a clear, living agreement about which decisions belong to which roles, at which level, with what input from whom. Here's a practical test: if you stopped any mid-level leader in your organisation and asked "Who decides X?", could they answer without hesitating? In most organisations, the honest answer is no — and that ambiguity is where accountability dies. The simplest way to create this clarity is through aligning the OKRs, which we'll discuss in the next section.

The companion piece is governance that actually governs. Chapter 11 diagnosed the disease: forums that exist to validate rather than challenge, where the real decisions happen in pre-meetings and hallway conversations, and the formal session is staged. The cure isn't more governance — it's better governance. It requires forums where the purpose is to discuss, debate, and make a decision. It means agendas structured around decisions rather than updates. And it means a culture where the forum chair's most important job is to ask: "What decision are we making today?" and "Does everyone understand what we are collectively committing to?"

The showcase approach from Chapter 6 — where teams present recommendations and proceed unless objections are raised — is one of the most effective governance models for this. It shifts the onus from teams seeking permission to leaders providing feedback and challenge, which dramatically improves both pace and ownership. It won't work for every decision (you wouldn't run a major acquisition this way), but for the vast majority of organisational choices, it beats the approval-seeking rituals most companies default to.

Governance That Gets Out of the Way

A market-leading organisation was embarking on a major project that was significantly more complex than anything it had delivered before. The project team had a concern. The governance processes that served them well in their core business, formal sign-offs, structured approval gates, escalation protocols, risked becoming the bottleneck on a project of this scale and pace.

At one of the first steering committees, the team made a radical proposal to the group executives overseeing the project. They would only seek formal approval for the most consequential decisions: those that materially affected delivery timelines, budgets, or the project's underlying economics. Everything else, design choices, tactical trade-offs, implementation sequencing, would be decided by the project team. However, every call would be made fully transparent to the Steering Committee, with a short window to raise objections or provide feedback. No objection within the window meant the decision stood.

This was a fundamental departure from how the organisation had always operated. Historically, most project decisions flowed through formal endorsement cycles. Discomfort in the room was obvious. But the executives, to their credit, agreed to run it as an experiment.

The experiment quietly became the new norm. The project team moved faster, with full accountability and full transparency. The Steering Committee found that it could focus its limited time on the handful of calls that genuinely needed executive judgement rather than rubber-stamping dozens of decisions it had no reason to second-guess. In the hindsight, it was a no-brainer.

The group executives effectively applied the 1% principle to governance itself: die in the ditch for the decisions that matter, and get out of the way on the rest.

Build the muscle through practice

Decision-making is like any muscle: use it well, and it strengthens, neglect it and it atrophies. Most organisations invest heavily in building analytical capability — better data, better models, better tools — but invest little in building sound judgment under uncertainty. As a result, some organisations become exceptionally good at generating analysis and remarkably poor at using it to deliver outcomes.

The following three practices can help close the gap.

First, **decision post-mortems**. These are common when something goes wrong. But the muscle building happens when it is done consistently to review how significant decisions were made and what outcomes they delivered — good and bad. The questions are simple: What did we know at the time? What did we miss? What would we do differently with the same information — not with hindsight, but with the same incomplete picture we had then? The last question is the most important, because it separates judgment errors from outcome errors. A decision can be wrong and still have been the right call given what was known. Equally, a decision can work out fine despite being poorly reasoned — and if you don't examine it, you learn nothing.

Second, **real-time coaching**. The most teachable moments in decision-making don't happen in training rooms. They happen in meetings, when a team is wrestling with a real problem under real constraints. Leaders who use these moments to help teams reframe questions, shine the light on hidden assumptions, and distinguish between what they know and what they're guessing build capability far faster than any formal training course. The discipline is to coach rather than direct. It requires asking the right questions such as: What are you actually optimising for? What are your underlying assumptions? What risks are you trying to mitigate? What needs to be true for this recommendation to stand? Rather than, "Here's what I'd do". Guidance through the right coaching-style questions builds the decision-making muscle within the team. Handing out an answer creates dependency.

Third, **celebrating the learnings and uncomfortable decisions**. Most recognition systems reward outcomes. We rightfully celebrate when we hit targets, deliver projects on time, sign a deal, grow revenue. However, very few organisations reward the quality of the decision process itself or the learnings from mistakes. An organisation that publicly celebrates a well-reasoned "no", such as a project killed because the evidence didn't support it, despite months of sunk effort, sends a far more powerful signal about decision-making culture than any number of town hall pep talks about "empowerment". Similarly, acknowledging a bold pivot — "we changed course because the data told us to, and that took courage" — normalises the behaviour you actually want. When organisations have courage to showcase both their "wins" and equally "learnings", it creates a culture where people are capable of making bold and fast-paced choices.

When Winning Is the Only Story Told

A large organisation ran monthly showcases where teams presented their achievements. The positivity was prolific. If you believed the presenters, the company was scoring goals left and right. But enterprise performance metrics told a different story. They were stubbornly flat. So was the appetite for risk. Teams gravitated towards safe, predictable initiatives and steered clear of anything that wasn't straightforward.

Two senior leaders decided to break the pattern. They took a showcase slot and, in front of the whole organisation, unpacked three of their own major stuff-ups from the previous two years. A new distribution channel pilot that delivered nothing but headaches. A marketing campaign that turned out to be a complete waste of time and money. And a digital feature launch that succeeded beyond expectations — only to overwhelm the platform and cause a serious outage.

They distilled the learnings from each, without sugar-coating or blame-shifting. It was the first honest showcase the organisation had seen. Over time, it became the norm. Teams started sharing what didn't work alongside what did. Learning from mistakes began to be valued rather than hidden. With that shift, bolder bets followed — and so did more honest conversations about performance, which improved as a result.

Codify without bureaucratising

In pursuit of institutional discipline, many organisations overcorrect well into process theatre territory. If good decision-making practices work, the instinct to codify is understandable. The desire is often genuine — to make something replicable by documenting the processes, training people on them, and measuring compliance. This desire comes from century-old management practices, designed for an era when the goal was to optimise the speed of a conveyor belt rather than the quality and pace of decision-making in a highly complex and ever-changing environment.

The problem is that by trying to reduce the art of decision-making to a checklist, we are at risk of replacing thinking with compliance. Instead, we should aim to build a shared understanding of what good looks like. This understanding will guide behaviours without constraining the creative thinking. It does not mean that processes and checklists are no longer required. In many circumstances they can be useful and even necessary, but be careful not to strangle your business with those.

Without trying to be exhaustive, here are three things that can help.

Align on a common language. When everyone in the organisation understands what "1% decision" means, or what "one-way vs two-way door" refers to, or what working through the "real options table" involves, the conversations become faster and more precise. You don't need to explain the framework every time — you invoke it, and people know what level of rigour the situation demands and what the next step is.

Share real stories. The internal folklore of choices that played out well and choices that didn't, told honestly and without sanitising them, is incredibly powerful. Stories travel faster than policies and resonate longer than online training modules. An organisation where people can say "Remember the X decision?", and everyone understands the lesson, has a strong decision-making culture.

Maintain rituals that reinforce without suffocating. A standing agenda item in leadership meetings that asks "What's the hardest decision we're avoiding?", a quarterly review of decisions made and outcomes observed, a habit of naming the decision tier at the start of every significant discussion. These are lightweight, but they keep the discipline visible and alive.

Incentive Alignment

Chapter 11 identified misaligned incentives as one of the most corrosive forces undermining decision quality. These misalignments come in various shapes and sizes: different teams optimising for different objectives, reward systems that punish course correction, promotion cultures that value confidence over accuracy. The obvious problem is that these make individual decisions harder, but more importantly they make the system produce predictably poorer outcomes, regardless of how talented the people operating within it are.

Fixing this issue is one of the toughest challenges in this entire book, because incentives are deeply embedded in how organisations measure performance, allocate resources, and promote people. But a few practical shifts make a material difference.

Start with **aligning objectives across the organisation**. Chapter 8 showed how OKRs frame individual decisions. Here the challenge is system-wide: do the OKRs across your organisation actually point in the same direction? This sounds like a strategy problem rather than a decision-making problem, but in practice the two are inseparable. When different teams are optimising for different, and sometimes contradictory, objectives, the result is not just annoying incoherence but a steady stream of unresolvable decisions or reluctantly accepted decisions that end up being undermined during implementation.

If you see the sales team pushing for volume at all costs while the product team is protecting margins or the digital team pushing new features while the operations team resists in order to avoid call-centre handling time pressure — these aren't incompetent people making bad calls. They are a manifestation of people making rational calls while optimising against misaligned scorecards. The fix starts at the top.

OKRs need to cascade from the CEO down with enough coherence that when two teams sit down to make a joint decision, they are at least solving for the same outcome even if they disagree on how to get there. Where objectives genuinely compete, that tension needs to be surfaced and resolved at the level above, not left for the teams to fight over in every meeting.

Then **align authority with accountability**. This sounds embarrassingly obvious but is violated constantly: whoever carries responsibility for a set of OKRs must also carry the decision-making authority related to them. Responsibility without authority is a recipe for frustration, resentment and learned helplessness. In practice, this means tracing your key objectives through the organisation and asking at each level: does the person accountable for this outcome actually have the authority to make the calls that determine it? If the answer is no, you've found a misalignment that no amount of goodwill or cross-functional collaboration can reliably overcome.

The challenge gets more nuanced with shared OKRs, which are common in modern complex organisations where outcomes genuinely depend on multiple teams collaborating. The temptation is to assign joint ownership, but joint ownership without a clear primary owner is really no ownership at all. It means that when trade-offs arise, and they always do, there is no one with both the mandate and the accountability to make the call. Every shared OKR needs a single person who carries primary responsibility, with other contributing teams having an important voice, but not being co-pilots. This primary ownership approach doesn't diminish the importance of working together. It simply ensures that when collaboration alone can't resolve a tension, there is absolute clarity on who makes the final call.

The next shift is to **reward the quality of the decision process**, not just the outcome. This sounds obvious until you try to implement it. Most performance systems are built entirely around results — revenue growth, delivery timelines, customer net promoter scores. These metrics matter, of course. But a leader who made a well-reasoned, well-informed decision that didn't work out due to factors outside their control has demonstrated more valuable judgment than a leader who got lucky on a poorly reasoned bet. If the performance system can't distinguish between the two, it's incentivising luck over skill. The people across the organisation will learn it fast and start optimising for what gets rewarded.

Ensure that **course correction is not penalised**. In many organisations, the act of killing a project or changing direction carries an implicit career cost. It looks like failure, even when it's the smartest thing you could do with the new information available. Create the conditions where people will actually change course when the evidence demands it. Set up funding models to allow reallocation without disproportionately punishing the write-off, refine governance structures to treat pivots as evidence of learning rather than evidence of poor planning, and get senior leaders to publicly endorse course corrections. These shifts can make significant progress towards normalising pivots and discouraging the habit of doubling down to avoid the stigma of admitting the original plan was wrong.

Finally, remember that **incentive alignment is never "done"**. Organisations evolve, strategies shift, and the incentive structures that were well-aligned two years ago may be counterproductive today. Ensuring incentive structures do what's intended is arguably one of the most important jobs for the board. The discipline is to periodically audit and fine tune the system by asking a question: "Are the behaviours we're rewarding actually the behaviours we need?" If the answer is "not quite", the incentive system may need adjustment, and ideally sooner rather than later when the drift becomes embedded.

Measure Decision-Making Quality

You can't improve what you don't measure, and most organisations don't measure decision-making at all. Companies measure outcomes obsessively: revenue, margin, NPS, delivery timelines. But these outcomes are lagging indicators that are functions of multiple factors such as decision quality, execution quality, market conditions, and luck. By the time an outcome is visible, the decision that produced it is months or years old, the context has been forgotten, and the lessons are buried under whatever crisis is demanding attention today.

If you're serious about building decision-making capability, you need to measure the process itself — not just what happened, but how it happened. The measure does not need to rely on scientifically proven methods — an honest self-assessment should do the job in most cases.

Like with any measurement, there are two types — lead and lag, and both are necessary. Lead indicators tell you whether the conditions for good decisions are in place before the outcome is known. Are the right people in the room — not too many, not too few, and with the right expertise and authority? Is genuine challenge happening, or is the forum turning into a talk fest to rubber-stamp predetermined choices? Are decisions being made at the right level, or are trivial choices consuming senior leadership attention while consequential ones get delegated? Is the decision framed correctly to focus on the right problem, or does the forum drift into answering a question no one actually asked? These are observable in real time, and they're fairly good at predicting decision quality.

Lag indicators tell you whether the decisions themselves are holding up. Did the decision produce the expected outcome within the expected timeframe? If not, was it because the decision was wrong, or because the execution was imperfect, or because the world changed in ways no one could have predicted? How long did the decision take relative to its complexity and consequence? Was the process proportionate, or did a Tier 3 decision consume Tier 1 resources? And critically: when circumstances changed and a decision required revisiting, did the organisation actually revisit it, or did it persist with a failing course because admitting the need for change felt too costly?

The practical mechanism doesn't need to be elaborate. A lightweight decision quality scorecard reviewed consistently, say quarterly, is more valuable than a sophisticated analytics dashboard that never gets used. The scorecard can cover a dozen or so of the most significant decisions made in that period. The scorecard questions can map directly to the six mortal sins from chapter 11:

The first two overarching questions relate to the relevant period of review, for instance the past quarter:

— Did we make important decisions consciously, or were there instances where we drifted into an outcome by default?

— When the evidence told us to change course, did we actually pivot, or were there instances where we doubled down to protect the original call?

The other four questions are decision-specific:

— Did we frame the right question, or did we spend our energy solving a problem that felt comfortable rather than one that mattered?

— Did we consider the right set of genuine alternatives, or did we miss some or worse, built a case around a predetermined answer?

— Did we decide at the right pace with the right level of information, or did we over-analyse past the point of diminishing returns?

— Did we commit clearly and unambiguously, or did we leave the room with "directional alignment" that no one followed through on, or that started relitigation?

Score your organisation or team 1-10 on each of the above, track trend over time, and patterns will emerge that no amount of outcome analysis alone would reveal.

The deeper insight here is one that Roger Federer's career illustrates beautifully. Over the course of his career, Federer won approximately 54% of the individual points he played. Barely better than a coin flip. Yet that marginal edge translated into winning roughly 80% of his matches and made him one of the greatest athletes in history. The lesson for decision-making is that you don't need to get every single call right. You need to get the important ones right more often than not, and you need to do it consistently, across the whole organisation, over the long term. That's what the measurement discipline creates — not perfection, but a system that regularly brings decision-making quality and discipline front of mind. This, over time, tilts the odds steadily in your favour, point by point, decision by decision.

When to Throw Out the Playbook

Everything in this book — the frameworks, the tiering, the governance, the cultural disciplines — is designed for the vast majority of decisions. But there are moments when the playbook doesn't apply, and the most dangerous thing a leader can do is cling to process when the situation demands speed and unilateral judgment.

It could be when the situation is so urgent that the leader needs to make a call and act immediately, or the information is so limited that no matter how long you analyse, the answer will be as good as a guess. A crisis is the obvious example, but it's not the only one. Sometimes a market window closes, a competitor makes a disruptive move, or the business gets hit by a major incident, and the elegant multi-stakeholder decision process you'd normally run is simply too slow for what the moment requires.

In these situations, the right move is to decide — clearly, quickly, and with whatever information you have. This is where all those small daily decisions pay off. The leader who has been practising FOCS for years will read the situation faster and make a better gut call than the one who has been coasting on hierarchy. But in these pressing situations, the real discipline is what happens after the call is made. The leader who decides unilaterally in an emergency needs to be clear about the call and own it unreservedly. There's no point dressing it up as a collaborative call or trying to share responsibility. The leadership standard is to manage reality and be honest. "I made this call without the usual process because the situation required it. Here's what I based it on. Here's what I was uncertain about. Let's review it in two weeks and see whether it was the right call".

When Crisis Helped Deliver a Year's Work in a Week

In the early days of the Covid pandemic, when isolated cases were starting to appear and panic was gradually setting in, but lockdowns had not yet started, a team of colleagues was having lunch at the office dining area. The leaders of the health insurer they were working for were grappling with what's coming and the profound impacts it will have on the business. The question that kept them up at night was whether the customers would start dropping their cover due to uncertainty.

One of the team members at the table was a data guru, who worked in audience analytics managing the email campaigns. He suggested that the health insurance customers must be confused and worried now, not knowing whether their policies cover Covid-19. Completely off the cuff, he said, wouldn't it be great if the customers were reassured that regardless of their level of product, the insurer will cover any hospital procedures directly related to Covid-19.

A colleague from strategy sitting across the table saw a Chief Marketing Officer walking past, pulled them in and asked his colleague to repeat what he just said. Slightly embarrassed by the unexpected limelight, the colleague shared his thought bubble about Covid-19 override concept that he's come up with a minute earlier.

The ten-second pause that followed felt like an eternity. Everyone stopped eating and looked at the CMO, who said: «You have no idea how good and timely this concept is.»

In normal circumstances a concept like that would have taken several months to explore, customer test, cost and business case. Under the unfolding Covid pandemic, they had to act fast.

And they did. It was high-level costed by actuaries overnight, submitted for executive approval the next day, and a week later the "Covid-19 override" was announced to customers giving them peace of mind that the insurer had their back in this pandemic no matter what product they were on.

They were the first to market to provide this assurance. They calmed the customer concerns. The exodus didn't eventuate even during the peak of the pandemic that followed.

It's a great example of brilliant ideas sparking in the least expected parts of the organisation and in the most unassuming circumstances. But more importantly, this is a stark illustration of the playbook being thrown out in the time of crisis and a new proposition rolled out to millions of customers in a week, rather than a year. The entire 50:1 Method compressed into a couple of senior leader conversations guided by the experience and a healthy dose of "gut feel".

The ability to act decisively and transparently in high-pressure circumstances does two things. It delivers the speed when it is genuinely needed. And it preserves trust, because the organisation sees that the exception was conscious and accountable. When these exceptions are visible, it actually proves that the discipline is working.

The goal should not be to religiously stick to the frameworks outlined in this book. It should be about building strong decision-making discipline within organisation and among its leaders. And sometimes it involves throwing out the playbook and following your gut. Do it purposefully and ensure that the exception doesn't, over time, become the norm.

Conclusion

We started the previous chapter with James Clear's observation that you fall to the level of your systems. The preceding sections have laid out what those systems look like in practice: leadership standards that model the behaviour you need, decision architecture that puts authority where it belongs, capability-building practices including guidance through coaching, incentives that reward the process as much as the outcome, and measurement disciplines that make decision quality visible before outcomes reveal it.

None of this is revolutionary — it is all common sense. And that's the whole point. Organisations don't struggle with decision-making because the solutions are unknown. They struggle because the mundane work of building the right habits, structures, and norms doesn't compete well against the next strategic initiative or the quarterly earnings cycle. Decision culture is like power, water, and sewage — largely invisible infrastructure that does wonders when it works, but catastrophic when it doesn't.

Companies can "buy" strategy by hiring management consultants. They can outsource execution to an offshore vendor. They can hire talent, acquire technology, and copy a competitor's product roadmap. But decision culture, which represents the collective ability of your organisation to identify what matters, choose well under uncertainty, commit fully, and course-correct without ego getting in the way, is the capability your competitors won't be able to easily replicate. It's built one decision at a time, by your leaders and your teams, in the daily meetings about matters that won't make it into Harvard Business Review articles.

The question, then, is not whether your organisation would benefit from better decision-making — that's a no-brainer. The question is what you, personally, are going to do about it. That's where we'll pick up in the epilogue.

Epilogue

"The best time to plant a tree was twenty years ago. The second-best time is now".

— CHINESE PROVERB

The Preface's "100% beer, 0% froth" promise deserves a bookend. You've made it to the end, which means that either I've kept that promise or you're a very determined reader. Either way, let's close the loop.

This book makes one argument: that decision-making is the highest-leverage activity in any organisation, and that most organisations don't treat it with adequate attention. We explored why a tiny fraction of decisions determines half of success, and why identifying your one percent «to die for» is the first and most influential act of leadership. We built a method around the Who, How, Why, and What, because getting any of those wrong produces a different flavour of failure and getting them right compounds. We made the case that culture, distilled into focus, openness, clarity, and speed, is not a backdrop for good decisions, but the operating system that produces them consistently. We mapped the mortal sins, the biases, the structural traps, and the quiet ego-driven viruses that corrode judgment. And we laid out the leadership standards and organisational practices that break these patterns. None of it is revolutionary. But all of it is hard.

It is hard, because the obstacle is not knowledge — you now have the frameworks, the diagnostic tools, and the practical disciplines. The real obstacle is follow-through on what needs to be done. And as we have seen, for many organisations a lot needs to be done differently. It's the difference between knowing the real question and actually bringing it up in a room full of people who'd rather not hear it. It's the difference between understanding that "no" is the right answer and saying it to a colleague who has invested months building a case. It's the difference between recognising that your team can handle a decision and actually letting go of it, even when muscle memory pulls you to lean in.

That gap is where the art lives. Decision-making is less science than art. . It can't be reduced to a model or a matrix, however much that would simplify things. It's a craft, built one decision at a time, through practice, honest reflection, and the willingness to be wrong in front of people.

In today's world, as AI tools become ubiquitous, every company will have access to similar data, similar models, and similar analysis. The raw material of decision-making is getting commoditised. I also expect that the 99% of choices are going to be increasingly automated. The raw material of decision-making is getting commoditised. I even foresee that the 99% of decisions are going to be increasingly commoditised. But when it comes to the 1%, you will still need top-notch "human intelligence". You can't commoditise the quality of framing, the courage to make a conviction-based call at 70% confidence, and the discipline to commit, execute, and hold the course when things get uncomfortable. In an AI-augmented world, the competitive advantage can no longer be sustained by reliable execution alone. It will increasingly require top-quality judgement, high-performing culture, and effective visionary leadership. That is what this book is about. It was true before AI, and it will be true as long as organisations are run by people.

The Roger Federer insight from chapter 12 is perhaps the most liberating idea in this book: you don't need to get every call right. You need to get the important ones right a little more often than not, and keep doing it. That's what separates good from great.

So, here's the million-dollar question: what will you do differently tomorrow — or even today, if you are reading this before lunch?

Not next quarter. Not at the next offsite. Tomorrow. When you walk into the first meeting of the day, will you ask "What's the real question we need to tackle?" Will you notice when the room is drifting toward a comfortable answer rather than the right one? Will you say "This is yours, I trust you", and mean it? Will you catch yourself optimising for optics, and choose to revert to substance instead?

You'll be exposed to dozens, if not hundreds, of these small daily choices. They don't feel like the 1% to die for. But they are exactly how decision-making culture gets built — one conversation, one meeting, one leader at a time, compounding until it becomes the way your organisation operates. No number of inspiring office posters and mandatory training sessions can shift the culture until those small daily choices that your leaders and people make start pointing in the right direction.

When these disciplines take root, something powerful happens: decision-making authority naturally cascades down the organisation. Leaders who trust the rigorous and transparent process become comfortable delegating more consequential choices closer to the work. The people who actually get stuff done stop being passive executors and become real decision-makers. That is when the method stops being a toolkit for the few and becomes an operating system for the many.

The ability to consistently make good calls under uncertainty, commit to them fully, and course-correct without letting ego get in the way is the essential capability that is very hard to build and equally hard for your competitors to replicate. The sooner you start, the greater the moat you'll build. Well, at least until AI takes over the world.

I set out to write a book with zero froth and no nonsense. You'll be the judge of whether I succeeded or failed miserably. But if even one idea from these pages changes the way you approach your next big decision, then the one percent I was aiming for has landed.

To paraphrase Jerzy Gregorek: Hard decisions, easy business. Easy decisions, hard business. The choice is yours.

Now go and make magic happen.

www.ingramcontent.com/pod-product-compliance
Lightning Source LLC
Chambersburg PA
CBHW051800050726
47598CB00006B/2364